EDITOR: Briony Quested

ART DIRECTOR: Nosca Northfield

FEATURES EDITOR: Kate Darcy

EDITORIAL: Kate Darcy, Dan Lewis, Nosca Northfield
Neil O'Rourke, James Stewart, Terence Teh

AREA FOREWORDS by: Styleslut (www.thestyleslut.com)

EDITORIAL CONTRIBUTORS: Zena Alkayat, Anna Bahow, Zephyr Bell
Sarah Bruce, Blair Cartwright, Harriet Compston, Gemma Croft
Sue Cruse, Esther Firman, Lisa Horton, Carolyn McBain, Mikki Most
Victoria Powell

PHOTOGRAPHY: Billa (www.shitbilla.com); Che Blomfield
(www.hellocheech.com); David Brook (www.davidbrook.co.uk); Ian Cox
Dean Chalkley (www.deanchalkley.com); Simian Coates
(www.coatesphotography.com); Exceedingly Good Keex; Lucia Graca
(www.luciagraca.com); Cade Hannan @ Garysh Productions
(www.garysh.co.uk); Nik Hartley (www.nikhartley.co.uk); Dave Hoyland
Jackson Kid; Fatsarazzi (www.fatsarazzi.co.uk); Ollie McFaul; Naughty
James (www.naughtyjames.com); Morgan O'Donovan; Grace Pattison
(www.gracepattison.com); Pure Evil (www.pureevilclothing.com); Rick
Pushinsky (www.pushinsky.com); Suk-ju Ryu; Ben Speck; Guy Stephens
(www.guystephens.com); Ed Whatling; Mark Whitfield
(www.markwhitfieldphotography.com)

PRODUCED BY: Partners in Media Publishing Ltd
Studio 52
The Old Truman Brewery
91 Brick Lane
London
E1 6QL
T: +44 (0) 20 7655 0995
Email: info@pimpguides.com
www.pimpguides.com

Printed in Germany
ISBN 978-3-7913-3884-2

PUBLISHED BY: Prestel Verlag, Munich, Berlin, London, New York

Prestel Verlag
Königinstrasse 9
D-80539 Munich
Germany
T: +49 (89) 242 908-300
F: +49 (89) 242 908-335

Prestel Publishing Ltd
4 Bloomsbury Place
London
WC1A 2QA
England
T: +44 (0) 20 7323 5004
F: +44 (0) 20 7636 8004

Prestel Publishing
900 Broadway, Suite 603
New York, NY 10003
Unites States of America
T: +1 (212) 995 2720
F: +1 (212) 995 2733
www.prestel.com

Prestel Books are available worldwide. Please contact your nearest
bookseller or one of the above addresses for information concerning your
local distributor.

British Cataloguing-in-Publication Data: A catalogue record for this
book is available from the British Library. The Deutsche Bibliothek holds a
record of this publication in the Deutsche Nationalbibliografie; detailed
bibliographical data can be found under: http://dnb.ddb.de

Library of Congress Control Number: 2008927139

Cover Photography by Exceedingly Good Keex; Model: Akiko of Comanechi / PRE

*Inside Cover Photography (from top, L-R): 01 & 02 Billa; 03 Eine; 04 & 05 Billa; 06 Keex; 07 & 08
Billa; 09 Keex; 010 Concrete Hermit; 011 Che Blomfield; 012 Billa; 013 Courtesy of 172; 014 &
015 Billa; 016 Che Blomfield*

*Inside Back Photography (from top, L-R): 01 Che Blomfield; 02 Ed Whatling; 03 & 04 Che
Blomfield; 05, 06 & 07 Billa; 08 Che Blomfield; 09 & 010 Billa; 011 Che Blomfield; 012 Keex; 013
Billa; 014 Che Blomfield; 015 Grace Pattison; 016 Che Blomfield*

Facing Page: Scarlet wears CHARLES OF LONDON; photography by Billo

CONTENTS

EAST LONDON

CENTRAL LONDON

NORTH LONDON

SOUTH LONDON

WEST LONDON

INTERVIEWS

How to use this book

OVERVIEW: If you haven't already noticed, London is a complicated beast. Like any self-respecting metropolis, it's in a constant state of flux. Areas rise in prominence, culturally and economically, only to fade as other boroughs and postcodes find favour and become fashionable. It's a cycle observed in cities across the globe and in the differing density of the sections of this book: East and Central compared with West and South. This is the present distribution of retail, entertainment and cultural production in London, as it relates to the young and style-conscious. The result, while seemingly weighted in favour of certain areas, is the highly functional, accurate and comprehensive guide you hold in your hand.

NAVIGATION:
The book has been divided into five sections: East / Central / North / South / West. The sprawling individual neighbourhoods of London are too numerous to start divvying up by their longitudinal positioning. And besides, we jump about a lot, spurning entire sections of the map to bring you only the best happenings in London. For an insight into each area, and our recommended neighbourhoods, see the forewords by London blogger, Styleslut: East (page 11) / Central (page 61) / North (page 109) / South (page 127) / West (page 135).

It's easy to become bogged down in semantics when trying to delineate London's various regions. The lines of demarcation are blurred to say the least. Usually, it falls to individual preference as to the terminology used to distinguish one area of the city from the next. Rather than singular tags, there's a pool of accepted references that most Londoners agree on. This is how it breaks down:

CATEGORIES

Within each area section, there are categories covering:

- ■ Bars & Clubs
- ■ Shopping
- ■ Art & Culture

For easy reference, area maps are provided at the back of the book, marking the reviewed venues.

LONDON AREAS

EAST:
Hoxton & Shoreditch / Hackney Dalston / Clerkenwell & Farringdon

CENTRAL:
Soho / Mayfair / Covent Garden Chancery Lane

NORTH:
Angel & Islington / Camden & Chalk Farm / Holloway / Kilburn Highgate

SOUTH:
New Cross & Deptford / Brixton Greenwich

WEST:
Notting Hill / Fulham & Chelsea Kensington / Shepherd's Bush

INTRODUCTION

Welcome to this book, and more importantly, welcome to London; we think you're going to like it. Well, we're assuming it's your intention to have fun, otherwise you'd be reading one of the more, shall we say, conservative guides out there. Designed for the sole purpose of helping savvy globetrotters like you get a taste of the real London, we've traversed boroughs, side-stepping the dull stuff, to bring you a highly-edited selection of fashion, music, art and culture venues. This off-the-map London is usually reserved for those who live here or are fortunate enough to have a clued-up, initiated friend to show them around. Well, we're that friend. And we fit in your bag! Sit back, relax and be informed, as we help you plan an altogether crazier time in *Old London Town.*

ABOUT US

We publish the most luxurious free magazine on the market — a hardback collectable style and street culture title that's available every two months at many of the venues featured in this book. Our artist agency represents some of the world's biggest and best contemporary and street artists (whose work you can buy at our online store). We also throw parties, art exhibitions and music events. We sometimes open temporary retail stores and art galleries in London, and then there's our seasonal live street art auction, Evolving Styles which features world-famous artists like Lady Pink, Faile, Blek le Rat, Nick Walker, DAZE and many more. Visit our website at www.pimpguides.com where you can access the latest news and London listings, view our store, and download digital editions of our magazine. For auction dates, see www.evolvingstyles.com

PURE EVIL artist / gallery owner

Q: What's the strangest thing that has happened to you in London while bombing the streets? I got chased down the street by a really pretty woman in high heels and a mini skirt. Turns out she was an undercover policewoman. Awesome! **Q: What's the one thing about London you couldn't live without?** The shitty oxygen mixed with car dust and small bits of metal that all Londoners breathe. **Q: Someone arrives in London for only 4 hours and you are their guide. Where do you take them?** I take them on a quick tour of the East End, pointing out all the street art. **Q: What's your favourite London store?** Maplins — a great place to buy electrical goods. **Q: And your preferred London gallery?** Pure Evil gallery, I spend my whole life here.

East

To many, east London is a big black hole waiting to consume anyone that dares to venture near its mouth without looking like they've been made over by **Jeremy Scott** and groomed by an asymmetrically-inclined Vidal Sassoon 'hair-technician'. Paying attention to your stylistic swagger is paramount, which is why we love the place so fucking much. Walk through Shoreditch on any given day and you'll be treated to a cornucopia of **creativity** and style that **Vogue** would die to document. But, these kids are so far ahead of the game that they would have passed them twice by the time the trend was published. Don't get it twisted though, the revolution isn't shallow. These creative parents give birth to **amazing music, style and art** offspring alongside all the party and bullshit. Whether throwing sartorially-edged shapes sharp enough to cut your throat at Hoxton's now-defunct Boombox or throwing 'gun-fingers' while gully **grime MCs** spray their latest bars at **Dirty Canvas,** east London knows what time it is and isn't afraid to embrace the unknown. Where else could **Dylan Mills** step out of his Bow council estate and morph into the Rascal that climbed **Big Ben** and eventually took over the world? It's that same attitude and foresight that pushes young designers to grab a sewing machine and flaunt their wares at **Spitalfields'** legendary market. Or make that fella with 'that haircut' start a band and play a gig in an elegantly dishevelled pub. DIY has never felt so good.

12
east london
bars & clubs

UNARGUABLY the hub of London's best nightlife, other areas of London are beginning — or at least trying — to claw some of the 'cool' back from east London, but nothing of any real significance yet. Regardless of the naysayers who love to chastise the 'vacuous hipster-populous' (as they see it), the East remains peerless in its concentration of great bars, clubs and pubs, squeezed into such a disproportionately small area.

333 + Mother   001

333 Old Street, EC1V 9LE
020 7739 5949
www.333mother.com
Tube: Old Street. Open: (333) Fri 22:00-02:30, Sat 22:00-05:00
(subject to change); (Mother bar) Mon-Sun 20:00-02.30

An East End institution, the 333 club has been at the centre of Shoreditch nightlife since the area's metamorphosis in the early-nineties. 333, and its late night appendage, Mother bar, are still home to some of the capital's most eclectic and forward-thinking club and gig nights, and have been a focal point of cool for over ten years — trust us, that's a long time in east London.

A10 Russian Bar   003

267 Kingsland Road, E2 8AS
07809 425905
www.russianbar.co.uk
Open: Sat 20:00-05:00

An after-hours drinking den in the truest sense. Villains and other dodgy characters rub shoulders with hipsters, clueless piss-artists, freaks and other waifs and strays keen to prolong intoxication. The clientele is an undoubtedly weird mix, but this is part of its appeal. Regularly used as an after-party venue, once you're in, you literally have no idea when you'll come out again. It's utterly insane.

93 FEET EAST   002

150 Brick Lane, E1 6QL
020 7247 3293
www.93feeteast.co.uk
Tube: Liverpool Street. Open: Mon-Thu 17:00-23:00
Fri 17:00-01:00, Sat 12:00-01:00, Sun 12:00-22:30

One of the most respected clubs in the area, 93 Feet East has established itself as an important spot on the unsigned and up-and-coming band circuit. Occupying a portion of the cavernous Old Truman Brewery complex in the middle of Brick Lane, the bar, club and gig venue has the most exciting emerging bands playing live every night of the week, and draws the biggest DJs, acts and promoters from across the globe. A creative hangout with regular art events and film screenings, the venue also has a cobbled courtyard with outside seating and BBQs in the summer.

Bar Music Hall

134 Curtain Road, EC2A 3AR
020 7613 5951
www.barmusichall.com
Tube: Old Street
Open: Mon-Thu & Sun 11:00-00:00
Fri & Sat 11:00-02:00

A huge cafe/bar housed in a Grade II-listed Victorian warehouse, playing host to club nights like FOR3IGN! which has a Saturday night residency here. You'll find a chilled vibe midweek with punters enjoying the Belgian beers on offer. Come the weekend, the promoters flood in to transform the venue into a haven for London's club kids. The bar serves food daily (to eat-in or takeaway), with a menu comprising burgers, roast dinners, breakfasts and snacks so it's a popular hangout for locals on Sunday afternoons.

Bardens Boudoir

38-44 Stoke Newington Road, N16 7XJ
020 7249 9557
www.bardensbar.co.uk
Rail: Dalston-Kingsland
Open: Daily 20:00-02:00

Hipper-than-thou, dirty little dive bar squeezed beneath an old carpet shop in Dalston. Sounds great doesn't it? That's because it is. Playing host to some of the capital's coolest club nights, this debauched little hide-hole deals in only the latest and greatest underground sounds, and comes complete with late licence, meaning the carnage goes on well into the early hours and beyond. Painfully hip, but then so many great nights out in London are. Trust us, you'll love it.

BETHNAL GREEN
WORKING MEN'S CLUB 006

44-46 Pollard Row, E2 6NB
020 7739 7170
www.workersplaytime.net
Tube: Bethnal Green
Open: Times vary

How and why this place is such a hipster haven is a little confusing at first glance, but remember this is precisely the reaction the kooky merchants of ironic cool like to illicit in plebeians like you. Don't worry I'm just kidding, I'm sure you're cool too. It's a working men's club anyway — the weathered 70's décor won't allow you to forget that, but herein lies the hook. It is what it is; a rudimentary bar serving drinks at reasonable prices — a miracle in itself these days. Combine this with an array of cabaret, burlesque, bands and other weird and wonderful themed parties and you have yourself one of the most unique and downright fun nights out in London.

CARGO 007

83 Rivington Street, EC2A 3AY
020 7739 3440
www.cargo-london.com
Tube: Liverpool Street
Open: Mon-Thu 18:00-01:00, Fri & Sat 18:00-03:00, Sun 18:00-12:00

Excelling as bar, club, restaurant and live gig venue, Cargo has all your night-out boxes ticked. Built into arches beneath a railway line, it's akin to drinking in a bomb shelter, but in a good way. There's also a nice decked outdoor area (heated, of course) so the fun can go on inside and out, and with listings that run the entire gamut of musical genres and stylings, there is always something worth checking out. Attracting a nice cross-section of party-goers, Cargo has a refreshingly unassuming and unpretentious crowd. Worth noting is the Cargo yard which doubles as a graffiti spot. In addition to art events throughout the year, the walls present the artwork of Banksy, Nick Walker, Faile and Shepard Fairey.

CAT & MUTTON 008

76 Broadway Market, E8 4QJ
020 7254 5599
Rail: London Fields BR
Open: Mon-Thu 12:00-23:00, Fri & Sat 12:00-01:00

Every few years, one pub in east London becomes 'the place to be and be seen'. Almost overnight, once sleepy boozers start attracting TV presenters, pop stars and assorted hipsters in their droves. The Cat and Mutton is one such pub; its recent boom in popularity reflective of Hackney's ongoing gentrification. With a superb, if slightly pricey, gastro menu, this stylish pub's kitchen is its main selling point, attracting a mix of local drinkers and diners throughout the week. The weekends, however, draw an entirely different crowd. From Friday to Sunday, this pub turns into one of the coolest spots in town, with the kids flocking from all over London for a pint.

CATCH 22 009

22 Kingsland Road, E2 8DA
020 7729 6097
www.thecatchbar.com
Tube: Old Street. Open: Tue & Wed 18:00-00:00
Thu, Fri & Sat 18:00-02:00, Sun 19:00-01:00, Mon closed

One of Shoreditch's consistently great nights out, Catch 22 is a bar, live music venue and club, trading in down and dirty-indie-rock 'n' pop. It's the type of place you're just as likely to see bands drinking as you are playing, ensuring a large number of beautiful hangers-on and try-hards, but that's unavoidable in a place like this. The downstairs bar is punctuated with intimate booths and sofas; getting one, however, is another matter as it's usually standing room only. Upstairs, the surprisingly roomy (when you consider the compact bar beneath) gig/club space is where you'll find nights of dirty electro glam, like FFUSS and Girlcore or alternatively, Indiesexual, for the best new rock and roll talent.

Opposite: THE PETER BLACK GROUP at FFuss @ Catch 22; photography by Billa

The **Dolphin**

165 Mare Street, E8 3RH
020 8985 3727
Rail/Tube: Hackney Central tube / London Fields BR
Open: Mon-Thu & Sun 11:00-02:00, Fri & Sat 11:00-04:00

If truth be known, this pub wouldn't be your first stop for a quiet afternoon pint with mates. Languishing in the no-mans-land that is Mare Street, The Dolphin's unique-selling-point is its late licence. By day, it's a frankly below-par boozer; by-night, however, it's just about the most debauched drink-hole you are likely to find anywhere. After midnight, when the queues start forming, bouncers vacuum-pack punters in — an experience which can only be likened to drinking on a rush hour tube. That said, you can't complain when you're supping pints at two-thirty in the morning. Due to its peerless after-hours status in the area, the place is heaving with the weird and wonderful from miles around; even the huge decked outdoor area is filled-to-bursting whatever the weather. Always good for a laugh, we end up here a lot.

By day, a frankly below-par boozer; by-night, it's just about the most debauched drink-hole you are likely to find anywhere

FOR3IGN! at Bar Music Hall; photography by Billa

DreamBagsJaguarShoes 011

34-36 Kingsland Road, E2 8DA
020 7729 5830
www.jaguarshoes.com
Tube: Old Street. Open: Tue-Sun 17:00-01:00, Mon 17:00-12:00

The bar's delightfully nonsensical namesake is taken from the retailers who previously occupied the property — exemplifying Shoreditch's transformation from impoverished warehouse wasteland to epicentre of London cool. Dream-Bags is chilled in the week and then like most bars in Shoreditch, rammed on the weekend. It's a no-frills type affair (in no way a bad thing) set over two floors: the upstairs bar doubles as a permanent gallery space, showcasing work from established artists, while the intimate downstairs bar is perfect for boozy evenings. Its music policy revolves around anything that's good, usually supplied by local heads and bar staff — simple but effective.

Electricity Showrooms 012

39a Hoxton Square, N1 6NN
020 7739 3939
www.electricityshowrooms.co.uk
Tube: Old Street. Open: Sun-Thu 12:00-00:00, Fri & Sat 12:00-01:00

One of the original Shoreditch drinking holes, the 'Showrooms' has been through a number of facelifts and name changes in recent years. Not quite the happening it once was, the bar now works more as a convenient place to grab a few drinks before moving on, located, as it is, slap bang in the centre of Shoreditch. It's a good spot though, and you will invariably end up in here at some point, if only due to its proximity to all the other local bars and clubs. Worth checking out is Wednesday night's Sing-A-Long where you can hit the basement's light-up disco floor to belt out karaoke.

CLUB PROMOTER & BLOGGER

Q: If you were the Mayor of London, what would you change? *"We'd reduce the crime rate and make every Friday 'National Krispy-Kreme Day'."* Q: What distinguishes London from every other city in the world? *"Too many people in a rush to go nowhere, red postboxes and Jodie Harsh."*

Fabric   013

77a Charterhouse Street, EC1M 3HN
020 7336 8898
www.fabriclondon.com
Tube: Farringdon
Open: Times vary but it's typically open till 5 or 7 a.m. at weekends

Love it or loathe it, Fabric's credentials as the global super-power of clubbing are without question. Expect the biggest DJs and acts from far and wide like The Cool Kids, Scratch Perverts, 2MnyDJs, Uffie, Diplo and Spank Rock. Boasting several rooms over two levels, the only valuable advice we can offer here is to get a lay-of-the-land and take note of what your friends are wearing *before* the drink kicks in, otherwise your chances of seeing them again are slim — the place is huge.

The George & Dragon   014

2 Hackney Road, E2 7NS
020 7012 1100
Tube: Old Street / Liverpool Street
Open: Daily 18:00-23:00

Don't be fooled by its shitty façade, The George and Dragon is the preferred haunt of the swathes of fashionistas who populate this part of town. We can't really tell you what to expect from this pub other than, if cliquishness doesn't sit well with you, you might want to consider your options — especially on a weekend. Haircuts from outer space and out-fits to match, geriatric cross-dressing DJs are the norm. An anything-goes party place and one of the area's liveliest.

Hoxton Bar & Kitchen   015

2-4 Hoxton Square, N1 6NU
020 7613 0709
www.hoxtonsquarebar.com
Tube: Old Street. Open: Mon 11:00-00:00, Tue-Thu 11:00-01:00
Fri & Sat 11:00-02:00, Sun 11:00-00:30

Many try, but few measure up to the grand-daddy of Hox-ton Square. One of the true originators in the area's now-legendary bar and club scene, the Bar and Kitchen has man-aged to transcend the East's notoriously mercurial tastes, setting the standard by which all others are judged — in recent times aided by the infamous club night, Boombox (R.I.P.). Crafted in clean lines of polished concrete, the bar has a timeless modernity which has undoubtedly aided its perennial chic. But within these stylised walls also lies great food and drink, and by night, a bleeding edge music pol-icy that has given the venue a reputation as 'the' harbinger of now sounds. Guaranteed to raise your cool rating by 10% per visit, expect to find models masquerading as bar staff, celebrities, hipsters, musicians — you get the picture.

The Macbeth   016

70 Hoxton Street, N1 6LP
0871 971 3890
Tube: Old Street
Open: Mon-Thu 11:00-01:00, Fri & Sat 11:00-02:00, Sun 12:00-00:00

Proving that location is far more important than presentation, The Macbeth's recent rebirth as a hip-destination required little more than moving the piss-soaked drunks that inhabited its darker corners, and giving the floor a quick mop. Now a live music, club and art gallery, The Macbeth plays host to some great club nights with live performances by bands and artists-of-the-moment. Commonly the music policy leans towards the indie/dance tip, but promoter nights can vary from cabaret to record label parties. One thing you're guaranteed is a welcoming energetic atmosphere. And whether you're visiting this venue in the day, or late-night, you can't fail to enjoy yourself.

The Old Blue Last   017

38 Great Eastern Street, EC2A 3ES
020 7739 7033
www.theoldbluelast.com
Tube: Old Street
Open: Mon-Wed 12.00-00:00, Thu & Sun 12.00-00:30, Fri & Sat 12:00-01:30

Best live music pub in London, end of story. Any bands worth their salt from the past few years, (Arctic Monkeys, Lily Allen, Klaxons) all played early shows here and with many regularly dropping in for impromptu gigs and DJ duties, there's a party most nights of the week. It's owned by Vice magazine, so there are industry connections at work here, guaranteeing consistently brilliant acts and nights. Refreshingly, you can still pop in for a quiet pint and read the paper during the day too. You can't come East and not check it out.

On the Rocks   018

25-27 Kingsland Road, E2 8DA
07961 363452
Tube: Old Street
Open: Wed-Sun 22:00-02:00

On the Rocks pumps out dirty electro and quality tech house, with live bands making the occasional appearance. Every Friday, London's longstanding club night, Trailer Trash takes over the venue, attracting a cosmopolitan crowd looking for upfront dance music. If you want to remove yourself from the main room, there is one escape route which leads to a long outdoor alleyway. Here, people socialise, smoke, gurn and flirt, before ending up back on the throbbing dance floor.

TOP & BOTTOM RIGHT: Victoria Park, Field Day Festival featuring Justice; photography by Che Blomfield

PARKS & GARDENS

HOXTON SQUARE / Tube: Old Street

To the uninitiated, this lacklustre patch of grass at the centre of Hoxton Square appears little more than a neglected public garden. However, to those familiar with the area, this tiny spot of strangled greenery represents something entirely different. Imbued with the spirit of nearly twenty years of progressive art, fashion, music and creativity, this little park has come to symbolise the beating heart of East End cool. During the summer months, the focal point of the area's entire social scene shifts, as drinkers replace the confines of the surrounding bars for cheap and cheerful al fresco boozing in the square.

VICTORIA PARK / Tube: Bethnal Green

Since the 19th century, this enormous space has been affectionately known as the 'people's park'. During the summer, locals flock to the park in droves, loaded with beer and barbeques, to enjoy an oasis of fish ponds, landscaped gardens and beautiful scenery. Victoria Park's famous reputation continues today, albeit on a grander scale, playing host to numerous music festivals including Lovebox and Underage Festival, which take place here every summer.

Plastic People

147-149 Curtain Road, EC2 3QE
020 7739 6471
www.plasticpeople.co.uk
Tube: Old Street
Open: Mon-Thu 19:30-00:00, Fri & Sat 22:00-03:30

An underground den for those with a deep respect for dance music. Plastic People's monthly Forward gig gave Dizzee Rascal's career a kick in the right direction and it continues to nuture London's finest home-grown acts. The venue adopts a no-frills approach to interior (fitting enough stripped wood to upset your average protester), and gives top priority to atmosphere with a sound system powerful enough to empty the most constipated bowel. Covering music across the board, it attracts a diverse line-up of promoters including secretsundaze who host occasional gigs here.

The Star of Bethnal Green   020

359 Bethnal Green Road, E2 6LG
www.starofbethnalgreen.com
Tube: Bethnal Green
Open: Mon-Thu till 00:00, Fri & Sat till 02:00

At the time of going to press, Rob Star (the acclaimed London DJ behind club night, Mulletover) has just opened the doors to his new venture — a traditional boozer and live music venue. Housed at the former site of Bethnal Green's Pleasure Unit, the two-floor site has been stripped out and had its original period features restored for its new incarnation as The Star of Bethnal Green. As with the Mulletover parties, expect the best in new music with a line-up of promoters and artists like Trailer Trash, Bugged Out! and Ali Love. A stage area previews live acts every Wednesday, and each night covers different genres from indie, electro and pop to disco and techno. The pub will feature live art by local street artists, and offer a jukebox, wireless Internet and food. Already attracting the area's hipster-elite, The Star looks set to do for Bethnal Green what the Old Blue Last has done for Old Street.

Ye Olde Axe   021

69 Hackney Road, E2 8ET
020 7729 5137
Tube: Old Street or Liverpool Street
Open: Sat 00:00-06:00

Evoking visions of a traditional English pub, Ye Olde Axe is anything but. By day through till early evening, the Axe is a strip club, but come late-Saturday night, it transforms into a den of inquity for indie kids, artists, local hipsters, 1950s-obsessed rockers, strippers, gangsters and randoms, united in their search of a late-night drink. Tattooed beauties jive to distorted retro rock 'n' roll that bleeds from the P.A. Rock-a-Billy Rebels is the current Saturday club night that causes all this commotion with its underground '50s soundtrack — the 7" tunes played are rarer than a sober person in this pub. This is London as one: drinking, dancing and lounging around talking bollocks. Some might say it's a dingy shit hole, we say it's one of the area's best after-hours spots.

LATE-NIGHT DRINKING

With most of the bars and pubs closing around 2a.m., what many visitors to London don't realise is, like many of our continental cousins, the UK now enjoys 24-hour licensing laws too. Let's be clear: there's never been a problem partying all night in London, we are, after all, home to the best club and music scene in the world. No, you just need to know where to go and which doors to knock on. What these new laws do mean, is that the number of establishments now willing and (legally) able to serve you alcoholic beverages at ungodly hours of the morning is increasing on an almost daily basis. The problem you kids are left with is which of these many after-hours locations are actually worthy of your time and your money, which is where we come in.

PHOTOGRAPHY

01 TOP LEFT: Trailer Trash at On the Rocks; photography by Billa, see page 20
02 TOP RIGHT: Bar Music Hall; photography by Billa, see page 15
03 MIDDLE LEFT: GIRLCORE at Plastic People; photography by Che Blomfield, see page 22
04 BOTTOM LEFT: GIRLCORE at Catch 22; photography by Che Blomfield, see page 16
05 BOTTOM RIGHT: Wet Yourself at Club Aquarium; photography by Billa, see page 27

WET YOURSELF at Club Aquarium; photography by Billa

Club Cool; photography by Billa

CAFE 1001

1 Dray Walk (off Brick Lane). E1 6QL. T: 020 7247 9679. Tube Liverpool Street. Open: Mon-Sat 06:00–00:00, Sun 06:00–23:30

Probably the most popular cafe/bars around these parts, 1001 is bustling with locals and out-of-towners morning, noon and night. Upstairs is a candle-lit den strewn with cushions and a cosmopolitan crowd enjoying the laid-back vibe, and there's a club in the back room which hosts live music and DJs, focusing on electro and drum 'n' bass. In summer, this place really comes into its own, with crowds spilling outside onto the picnic tables to drink beer and eat BBQ food.

APPROACH TAVERN

47 Approach Road, E2 9LY. T: 020 8980 2321. Tube: Bethnal Green. Open: Mon-Thu 12:00-00:00, Fri & Sat 12:00-02:00, Sun 12:00-23:00

The Approach Tavern is one of a cluster of great pubs in the Bethnal Green area. Set among the beautiful Victorian townhouses that line the Approach Road, it benefits from both a superb gastro menu and a large heated beer garden, meaning punters can drink inside and out all year round — which is good news for the smokers. Clientele is a fairly even mix: local cool kids and artists mix with young families and dog walkers in a relaxed and friendly atmosphere. Sunday lunches, like the pub itself, come highly recommended.

Big Chill Bar

Dray Walk, E1 6QL. T: 00 7392 9180. W: www.bigchill.net. Tube: Liverpool Street Open: Sun-Thu 12:00-00:00, Fri & Sat 12:00-01:00

A bar by the festival of the same name, this is chilled-out drinking for afternoon hangovers with DJ sets every Sunday.

Cafe 1001

See the review above.

The Camel

277 Globe Road, E2 0JD. T: 020 8983 9888. Tube: Bethnal Green Open: Mon-Wed 16:00-23:30, Thu-Sun 12:00-23:30

A tiny pub, honestly, it's Lilliputian in size, and if that wasn't enough, it resides at the end of an alley called Sugar Loaf Walk and serves magic pies. Seriously, go there and try the pies, they're amazing. Its size means it fills up really quickly, but don't let that stop you having a look.

The CARPENTER'S ARMS

135 Cambridge Heath Road, E1 5RN. T: 020 73776415. Tube: Liverpool Street Open: Mon-Thu & Sun 12:00-23:00, Fri & Sat 12:00-01:00

A pub steeped in history, The Carpenter's Arms was purportedly owned by notorious London gangsters the Krays, so they could have a safe pub to drink in. It has lost none of its old-time East End charm in its recent refit. With a great selection of exotic continental brews and micro-brewery beers and ales from around the world, the focus here is very much on the booze, and why not?

CLUB AQUARIUM

256-264 Old Street, EC1V 9DD. T: 020 7253 3558 W: www.clubaquarium.co.uk Tube: Old Street. Open: Times vary

A nightclub with an in-house swimming pool, this place's popularity is entirely dependent on the promoters who host parties here. With this in mind, the nights worthy of a visit are Sundays when the club kids pour in en mass for the dirty electro club, Wet Yourself, featuring Ed Banger DJs, and acts like Zombie Disco Squad (22:00-04:00). Saturday morning's Redlight Afterhours takes gig goers through till 11a.m. (starts at 04:30).

The Commercial Tavern

142-144 Commercial Street, E1 6NU. T: 020 7247 1888. Tube: Liverpool Street Open: Mon-Sat 17:00-23:00, Sun 12:00-22:30

Nice bar split over two levels. The interior has a crazy Louis XIV-meets-porno flick type vibe, which actually works, and there is also a pool table.

Dalston Jazz Bar

4 Bradbury Street, N16 8JN. T: 020 7254 9728. Rail: Dalston Kingsland Open: Mon-Thu 17:00-03:00, Fri & Sat 17:00-05:00, Sun 17:00-02:00

A nice little spot which is worth a visit if only for a late-night drinking session. Don't fantasise about a smoke-filled room and music from Billie Holiday though — it's not here. Expect more of a school youthclub vibe, but with adults.

The Dove

24-28 Broadway Market, E8 4QJ. T: 020 7275 7617. Rail: London Fields. Open: Mon-Thu & Sun 12:00-23:00, Fri & Sat 12:00-00:00

Huge, and we mean huge, selection of imported continental beers, with excellent food too. A great place to enjoy a pint or lunch if you're at the Broadway Farmers Market on a Saturday.

East Village

89 Great Eastern Street, EC2A 3HX. T: 020 7739 5173. W: www.eastvillageclub.com Tube: Old Street Open: Times vary

East Village introduces the best in rare and underground disco and house music at this new Shoreditch club. Wood floors, low lighting and exposed brickwork pay homage to the loft spaces of New York, while quality promoters ensure that artists like James Righton (Klaxons) and Matt Waites (Nightmoves) drop by for sets. The three-floor club also hosts Gilles Peterson's monthly residency, plus parties by Go!Zilla and Disco Bloodbath.

The Griffin

93 Leonard Street, EC2A 4RD. T: 020 7739 6719 Tube: Old Street. Open: Mon-Sat 11:00-23:00, Sun 12:00-22:30

A dishevelled pub in the heart of Shoreditch, The Griffin is everything a good local should be. With a pool table, decent jukebox, friendly bar staff, a great variety of beers and ales on tap, and DJs making regular appearances on the weekend, this is an essential spot for an afternoon of boozing.

Herbal

10-14 Kingsland Road, E2 8DA. T: 020 7613 4462. W: www.herbaluk.com Tube: Old Street Open:Wed-Thu 21:00-02:00, Fri & Sat 21:00-03:00, Sun 22:00-02:00

Set in an old brick and timber warehouse, Herbal blasts out a mix of leftfield, drum 'n' bass, nu-jazz, house and breaks most nights of the week, catering to a friendly crowd of underground music connoisseurs. It has one of the loudest sound systems in London and has played host to DJs such as Kool DJ Herc, Gilles Peterson and Roni Size (as well as the burgeoning talent). Herbal is hugely respected on the scene, so if dubstep and drum 'n' bass are your thing, then you can't go wrong here.

The Lauriston

162 Victoria Park Road, E9 7JN. T: 020 8985 5404 Rail: London Fields BR. Open: Mon-Thu 11:00-23:30 Fri-Sat 11:00-00:30

Lively and super-friendly pub serving the best pizza in east London. There's a free jukebox too. We love it.

Owl & Pussycat

34 Redchurch Street, E2 7DP. T: 020 7613 3628 Tube: Liverpool Street. Open: Times vary

Great pub, heated beer garden and legendary Sunday lunches.

Passing Clouds

Off 440 Kingsland Road, E8 4AA (to the rear of Uncle Sam's pub). T: 020 7684 0577. W: www.passingclouds.org. Rail: Dalston Kingsland. Open: Times vary

A new backstreet arts club in Dalston with a regular programme of art, film, theatre and music events in the pipeline. One to watch.

Passions

251 Amhurst Road, N16 7UN. Rail: Dalston Kingsland Open: (Disco Bloodbath: Monthly / Sat 22:00-06:00)

The monthly basement party, Disco Bloodbath is hosted at Passions featuring international DJ acts like Padded Cell, Horse Meat Disco and Rooty. Visit: www.myspace.com/discobloodbathdisco for dates.

Prague

6 Kingsland Road, E2 8DA. T: 020 7739 9110 W: www.barprague.com. Tube: Liverpool Street or Old Street. Open: Daily 10:00-00:00

Small and softly-lit, Prague bar offers the most intimate drinking experience in the East End. They specialise in Czech beers and cocktails and serve great coffee, cheeses and nibbles to a relaxed crowd of local artists and musicians.

Pub on the Park

19 Martello Street, E8 3PE. T: 020 7275 9586 Rail: London Fields BR. Open: Times vary

A short walk from London Fields station, Pub on the Park provides both a haven of tranquility throughout the week and a pre-club weekend jump-off. Salt-of-the-earth locals rub shoulders with east London bohemia to create a unique community atmosphere. In the summer, the pub buzzes with life, and London Fields becomes a mini festival. The air grows thick with barbeques, tunes and Hackney skunk, surreally juxtaposed against cricketers dodging drunkenly-propelled Frisbees.

Public Life

82a Commercial Street, E1 6LY. T: 020 7375 1631 W: www.publiclife.org.uk. Tube: Liverpool Street Open: Times vary

Starting life as a Victorian public toilet, this cramped, subterranean venue rarely closes on weekends. It's hired by a wealth of promoters and is a favourite haunt of the types of gurning loons you'd expect to find in a former shithouse. If staying up for 48 hours listening to nosebleed-techno is your thing, in you come!

GIRLCORE at CATCH 22; photography by Billa, see page 16

ISSUE MAGAZINE at Electricity Showrooms; photography by Billa, see page 18

The RED LION

41 Hoxton Street, N1 6NH. T: 020 7729 7920
W: www.redlionhoxton.com Tube: Old Street
Open: Mon-Sat 11:00-00:00, Sun 12:00-11:00

The founder of the 333 club offers Londoners another drinking den, this time in the form of a traditional boozer. The pub is set over three floors with DJs playing funk, soul and hip hop every night to an after-work crowd of Hoxtonites. Its greatest draw is the roof terrace which has sun loungers and picnic tables. There's a jacuzzi too, although it rarely works.

The REDCHURCH

107 Redchurch Street, E2 7DL. T: 020 7729 8333
W: www.theredchurch.co.uk Tube: Liverpool Street. Open: Mon-Thu
17.00-01.00, Fri & Sat 17.00-03.00, Sun 13.00-01.00

Great bar for grabbing a few drinks before moving on, located as it is on the thoroughfare linking Hoxton and Brick Lane. It's quite compact so fills quickly on a weekend, but it has a really nice selection of beers, so that's fine. Most notably, it serves the Aussie brew, Coopers Ale, which we have never seen anywhere else.

NUKE 'EM ALL; photography by Billa

RHYTHM FACTORY

16-18 Whitechapel Road, E1 1EW. T: 020 7375 3774. W: www.rhythmfactory.co.uk. Tube: Aldgate East. Open: Sun-Thu till 03:00, Fri & Sat till 06:00

Tribes of rock scruffians get it on with sweaty funkateers at this club, while A&R men clamber through the crowd, desperately trying to tag the next big thing. Rock gigs, funk sessions, poetry and comedy also feature, reflecting the Rhythm Factory's diverse arts policy. One of London's best grime nights, Dirty Canvas is often hosted here, showcasing the most promising artists of the genre.

The Royal Oak

73 Columbia Road, E2 7RG. T: 020 7729 2220. W: www.royaloaklondon.com Tube: Old Street. Open: Mon 18:00-23:00, Tue-Thu & Sun 12:00-23:00, Fri & Sat 12:00-00:00

This amazing pub on Columbia Road (the one with the big Sunday flower market), is right up there with our favourites in the area. The 1940s decor alone makes it worth a visit, but the place also serves up award-winning food and a decent range of booze. Even better, there is always a fair few bar staff, so you're not standing about waiting even when it's busy.

The T Bar

56 Shoreditch High Street, E1 6JJ. T: 020 7729 2973. W: www.tbarlondon.com Tube: Liverpool Street. Open: Mon-Wed 09:00-00:00, Thu 09:00-01:00, Fri 09:00-02:00, Sat 20:00-02:00, Sun 18:00-00:00

An old tea warehouse which has been converted into work spaces for the creative industries. A huge timer is presented at the front of the building counting down the hours until last orders, which is your only clue that this building doubles as a bar/club. Specialising in electronic and disco music, you'll find resident DJs like Gilles Smith playing one night, and Phonica Records appearing the next.

The Ten Bells

84 Commercial Street, E1 6LY. T: 020 7366 1721. Tube: Liverpool Street Open: Times vary

The public house allegedly frequented by a number of Jack the Ripper's victims, The Ten Bells drips with ye-olde-Dickensian charm. Retaining much of its Victorian interior, it's like having a pint in the olden days. Don't be alarmed if you see Queen Victoria, Sherlock Holmes or the man himself, Charles Dickens, popping in for a swift pint.

VIBE BAR

The Old Truman Brewery, 91 Brick Lane, E1 6QL. T: 020 7426 0491 W: www.vibe-bar.co.uk Tube: Liverpool Street. Open: Mon-Thu & Sun 11:00-23:30, Fri & Sat 11:00-01:00

Vibe is one of the original DJ bars in this area. Low lighting at all times of the day, deep red Chesterfields, slouchy sofas, gothic iron chairs, there's even Ron Jeremy and Linda Lovelace guiding you to respective toilettes. The music and atmosphere are provided by an array of genre-hopping DJs, VJs and live acts who perform here every night of the week. Any visit to Vibe is a laid-back affair, especially in summer when the large courtyard is taken over by a friendly crowd of students, suits, musicians and artists, drinking and enjoying the barbeque food that's on offer every night. Its new art gallery and upstairs bar should keep this place popular for years to come.

The White Hart

89 Whitechapel High Street, E1 7RA. T: 020 7247 1546. Tube: Whitechapel. Open: Mon-Wed 11:00-23:00, Thu 11:00-00:00, Fri & Sat 11:00-01:00, Sun 12:00-23:00

A nice spacious old boozer, The White Hart is a great place for watching the football, with plenty of large screens and a relaxed atmosphere. The small upstairs room is regularly used by local promoters for club nights. There are no permanent gigs to speak of, but it's always worth checking what's on if you're in the area.

ZIGFRID von Underbelly

11 Hoxton Square, N1 6NU. T: 020 7613 1988. W: www.zigfrid.com Tube: Old Street. Open: Daily 12:00-01:00

A spacious, bare brick bar and club with leather sofas and plush soft furnishings. It's popular with PR girls and design types who bump to a mixed bag of sounds — everything from late '60s psych to dancehall. The basement club, Underbelly is a dirtier spot featuring live gigs and DJs.

Q: **Where's your favourite place to eat out in London?** "LMNT resturant on Queensbridge Road. The food isn't that good (the meat's awful), but the starters are amazing, especially the goat's cheese. But fuck the food, this place is decorated like an Egyptian wendy house and they have great cocktails like Bleeding Cleopatra. If you book in advance, ask for a treehouse and you'll have a table in the skies." Q: **Best place to buy music?** "Second Layer Records." Q: **What do you think is London's most impressive landmark/attraction?** "The portal in Elephant and Castle roundabout. It's a huge box-like hypercube that various people have occasionally developed relationships with. James (Klaxons) once followed a fox off a bus and we both woke up there without the fox." Q: **Best place to see live music?** "Do people still go to 333? I heard it shut then reopened. I've been out of the loop. It has the most ridiculously stupid stage with a metal pole through the middle like a high jump. That place reminds me of the portal and being satisfied with catastrophe. Good times. I love The Forum for big shows." Q: **What's the best venue you have played in London and why?** "Brixton [Academy] is a living breathing dream. At the time, Madame JoJo's — it seemed bigger than Wembley. White Heat is a must for anyone experiencing linear time."

KLAXONS

Simon Taylor-Davies
GUITARIST

Photography by Keex

The East End offers the most trend-defining retail in London. A diverse, if geographically condensed, retail playground, it will sate both your designer and vintage shopping appetite. There's little in the way of high street 'essentials' over here, but if you're after obscure, small designers, choice vintage or high-end streetwear, then the East's where it's at. Better still, it comes in an easily navigated, square-mile bundle, so you won't be knackered after a day's shopping.

172   022

172 Brick Lane, E1 6RU
020 7650 8873
www.shop172.com
Tube: Liverpool Street
Open: Mon-Fri 12:30-19:00, Sat-Sun 11:00-19:00

172 is a style-obsessive's dream store. Hunting newcomer labels that sit at the rapier-sharp edge of fashion design, this place offers a heads-up on tomorrow's talent, specialising in Japanese labels and small, independent local designers. The labels stocked here are newborn but the quality of the garments in both design and finish is outstanding. The real beauty of 172 is the buying team's ability to identify exciting, fashion-forward designers, resulting in a brilliant selection of apparel and accessories. Many of the pieces lean towards the signature Japanese aesthetic in terms of cut and design, and it's one of the few stores in this area that focuses on this styling. Somehow, 172 has avoided the attention of the masses, but it is indelibly imprinted in every fashion lover's notebook.

Absolute Vintage   023/026

15 Hanbury Street, E1 6QR
020 7247 3883
www.absolutevintage.co.uk
Tube: Liverpool Street
Open: Mon-Sat 12:00-19:00, Sun 11:00-19:00

Leaning more in favour of the girls, Absolute Vintage is an Aladdin's cave of second-hand goodness specialising in UK and US clothing from the 1930s to 1980s. The first thing that strikes you upon entering is the staggering selection of shoes, which take up two entire walls of this huge store. Its impressive stock makes it a hunting ground for top design houses like Gucci, Missoni and DKNY who visit the store for research purposes. It's extremely popular due to its killer-no-filler stock, which means if you see something you like, grab it, because we guarantee it won't be there for very long. A little further along, on Commercial Street, you'll find Absolute Vintage's sister boutique, Blondie, which stocks posh vintage from the likes of Vivienne Westwood and Gucci.

BLONDIE: Unit 2, 114-118 Commercial Street, E1 6NF. T: 020 7247 0050

American Apparel   024

123 Curtain Road, EC2 A3BX. T: 020 7012 1112. W: www.americanapparel.net
Tube: Old Street. Open: Mon-Wed 10:00-20:00, Thu 10:00-21:00, Fri-Sat 10:00-20:00, Sun 12:00-18:00

A one-stop shop for all your fashion essentials, American Apparel's brightly-coloured hoodies, tees, sweats and accessories have become the casual staples of every style-conscious wardrobe in London. As well as being cheap and endlessly wearable, all their garments are ethically manufactured, so you can adorn yourself safe in the knowledge that they haven't been produced by an exploited child in the third world.

Beyond Retro

110-112 Cheshire Street, E2 6EJ. T: 020 7613 3636. W: www.beyondretro.com
Tube: Liverpool Street. Open: Daily 10:00-18:00

Less a shop than a warehouse, Beyond Retro is the unrivalled jewel in London's vintage shopping crown. With rack upon rack of constantly rotated and updated stock, there is a real danger you may lose a few days of your life in here sifting through the never-ending supply of garbs. The 5000 sq ft space stocks the largest selection of American vintage in Europe, dating from the 1940s onwards. Better still, Beyond Retro know they're trading second-hand goods and, defying the current trend for overpriced vintage, keep the prices low. Now a London fashion landmark, this place is an essential source of clothing, accessories and footwear for the capital's top stylists, and it even attracts local bands who perform live here on weekends.

Sample Sales

Ever wondered what fashion labels and designers do with all that product they don't sell? They have sample sales. Huge rooms filled with piles of marked-down clothing and accessories, where you can pick up items from last season or one-off samples for unbelievably cheap prices. They happen across London, but the best ones can always be found in the East End, usually in or around The Old Truman Brewery (Brick Lane/Dray Walk). You need to keep your eyes peeled when you're in this neck of the woods though, as venues rarely advertise the fact beyond an open doorway with a flyer stuck on the wall beside it. Missing them is easy; trust us, you'll kick yourself if you do. Like a year's worth of retail-therapy squeezed into one afternoon, you can usually spot the sales by the people drunk on bargains, staggering down the street, clutching their freshly-purchased designer goodies.

025

PHOTOGRAPHY
ABOVE: Beyond Retro photography by Keex
OPPOSITE: 172 photograph courtesy of 172
TOP LEFT: Blondie photography by Keex

GoldieLocks
RAPPER / SINGER / PRODUCER

Q: Someone arrives in London for only 4 hours and you are their guide. Where do you take them?
Firstly, I would go to get some grub! I just went to this wicked little pie and mash place off Carnaby Street called Mother Mash — you can choose what sausages you have, how your mash is made… it's sick (in a good way). Obviously, being at Carnaby Street, I would take them for a spot of shopping — I usually go to Kingly Court as there are some really cool vintage shops and you can find some bargains down there. Lastly, I would take them over to the Absolut Ice bar which is just off Regent Street. You get given a huge Santa Claus jacket and gloves and get taken into a freezing room where the bar, glasses, seats, everything is made from ice! Cool place. Literally. **Q: What's the best venue you have played in London?** I really liked playing at The Scala — there are loads of rooms so you can get a variety of music experiences within one night. It's good value for money and a well up-for-it crowd. **Q: Where's your favourite place to eat out in London?** I always go to this little Chinese place called Cafe TP in Chinatown. My friend from music college showed me it a few months ago and we haven't stopped going since! It's always busy there, which I think is a good sign! I recommend the sweet and sour chicken or char-sui pork. **Q: Favourite club(s) / nights?** I don't really go to all those poncy parties; I hate places where people spend more time looking at what each other is wearing than actually enjoying the music. I recently went to a place called Sugar Cane in Clapham Junction; it's a Hawaiian-themed bar with bamboo walls, reggae music and the most amazing cocktails. I don't really remember much after that. (Sugar Cane: 247-249 Lavender Hill. Tube: Clapham Junction).

Buckler   027

35 Artillery Lane, E1 7LP
020 7377 2767
www.andrewbuckler.com
Tube: Liverpool Street
Open: Mon-Fri 11:00-18:30, Sat 11:00-18:00, Sun 11:00-17:00

New York based designer, Andrew Buckler returns to his
British roots with a UK flagship of his cult Anglo/Amer-
ican menswear label, Buckler. Worn by everyone from Iggy
Pop to Agyness Deyn, the label is showcased in its entirety
at this store, which is situated at the former entrance to
Henry VIII's artillery grounds. You can also pick up the
Sexy Bastard range of clothing and footwear.

Buckler photography by David Brook

Gloria's photography by Nosca & Keex

Gloria's   028

Shop 6, Dray Walk, E1 6QL. T: 020 7770 6222. W: www.superdeluxe.net
Tube: Liverpool Street. Open: Daily 10:00-19:00

Taking its name from the Cockney rhyming slang, Gloria Gayner's, meaning trainers, this exquisite streetwear
boutique is two floors of rare gum and leather with exclusives and limited edition footwear from brands like Nike
and Adidas. Cabinets preview next season's samples, while
a fine collection of toys and clothing grace the shelves with
the same seal of quality as their kicks: deadstock Nike tees,
basketball vests, Stüssy and Obey apparel, and their glorious own-brand tees. The staff are friendly, helpful and
most importantly for sneaker-heads, knowledgeable.

Goodhood & Hoxton Boutique photography by Keex

Goodhood 029

41 Coronet Street, N1 6HD
020 7729 3600
www.goodhood.co.uk
Tube: Old Street
Open: Tue-Sat 11.00-19:00, Sun 12.00-17:00

A streetwear boutique of the highest order, Goodhood stocks a range of product you will be hard pushed to find in many other places in the UK: Perks and Mini (PAM), Sperry, WoodWood and Medicom Life, among others. Of course, you can also expect a plethora of other goodies and high-end accessories. In addition to the beautifully-presented retail store, the two-storey premises are also home to the Goodhood Gallery and Studio. The gallery space regularly showcases artists, illustrators, animators and designers from around the globe.

Hoxton Boutique 030

2 Hoxton Street, N1 6NG
020 7684 2083
www.hoxtonboutique.co.uk
Tube: Old Street
Open: Mon-Fri 10:30-18:30, Sat 11:00-18:00, Sun 12:00-17:00

A favourite of those who live around the East End, this is the place to pick up a piece by the brightest young fashion designers. Hoxton Boutique offers an outstanding selection of the best labels out there so it's a regular destination for London's clued-up shoppers. With the latest sounds roaring from the speakers and a disco ball shining overhead, the rails of desirable womenswear seem almost like an added treat. Some of the collections represented here include international designers like Hussein Chaylan, MM6, and Isabel Marant, as well as the boutique's own label, +HOBO+.

Hurwundeki 031

98 Commercial Street, E1 6LZ
020 7392 9194
www.hurwundeki.com
Tube: Liverpool Street
Open: Mon-Fri 11:00-19:30, Sat & Sun 10:00-19:30

HURWUNDEKI has a second store in Soho at 34 Marshall Street, W1F 7EU. T: 020 7734 1050

This little shop is full of surprises. While stocking a nice range of independent men's and women's designers and its own Hurwundeki label, downstairs in the cellar you will also find a grotto filled with choice vintage pieces and accessories from the Victorian period onwards. To top it off, nestled around the corner from the main shop, there is also HWDKI, a top hair salon where you can get a style to complement your new 1960s frock.

We asked **Junky Styling**
Q: Where serves the best breakfast?

"Hangover cure from Rossi's and E Pellicci's for leisure."

JUNKY STYLING   032

12 Dray Walk (off Brick Lane), E1 6RF
020 7247 1883
www.junkystyling.co.uk
Tube: Liverpool Street
Open: Daily 11:00-18:30

One of the most innovative fashion boutiques in London, Junky recycles old clothes and turns them into stunningly original and stylish garments. In contrast to the shoddy reworkings of many recycled clothing designers, Junky restyles with the utmost skill, creating designs fit for the catwalk of a top fashion house. Producing skirts and tops out of men's shirts and suits, and handbags out of an old pair of trousers, you won't find two of the same design anywhere in the world. Junky design for men and women and offer a customisation service in addition to the ready-to-wear collections. Due to popular demand for this service, there's a turnaround period of 2-3 weeks, so if the length of your visit prevents you from reinventing your wardrobe, buy something individual off-the-peg instead.

JUNKY STYLING Recommends:
Rossi's Cafe & Snack Bar: 8 Hanbury Street, E1 6QR
E Pellicci: 332 Bethnal Green Road, E2 0AG

Junky Styling photography by Keex

The Lazy Ones photography by Che Blomfield

The Lazy Ones 033

102 Sclater Street, E1 6HR
020 7729 6937
Tube: Liverpool Street
Open: Tue-Sun 11:30-20:00

Originally hailing from a rabbit farm in Spain, half siblings, Natalia Lolom and Diego Tellez launched this boutique and named it after their band, The Lazy Ones. It was a fake band. The reason being that neither Natalia nor Diego could play an instrument or sing. Be that as it may, they wrote the lyrics and melodies, have performed several London gigs and even recorded some of their tracks including '*I Wanna Have a Shop*'. Before opening the store, Natalia studied illustration at Central St Martins and her art now adorns the shoes, bags, sweats and shirts on sale in-store. While Natalia creates their own fashion label and chooses the unisex vintage for the boutique, Diego, who they admit is the more organised of the two, manages the shop. The space — which was decorated entirely by the duo — focuses on fashionable dresses, with an abundance of unisex sweats, shirts and US vintage on offer. Kate Moss, Gael Garcia Bernal, Kelly Osbourne and the like shop here. Oh, and it featured in Shoreditch TV satire, *Nathan Barley*.

lik + neon 034

106 Sclater Street, E1 6HR
07876 323 265
www.likneon.com
Tube: Liverpool Street
Open: Mon 12:00-19:00, Tue-Sat 11:00-19:00, Sun 11:00-18:30

There is more crammed into this bijou space than in a shop ten times its size. Specialising in all manner of collectable paraphernalia, the store is a treasure trove of limited-run clothing and jewellery from up-and-coming designers, prints, fanzines, alt-publications, art, CDs and other wonderful obscurities. Janice, the owner, regularly collaborates with artists to create store installations, most recently, with design collective Lo-Tec who transformed the shop into a pixellated Tetris block for London Design Week. A great independent store which encapsulates what Brick Lane is all about.

lik + neon photography by Suk-ju Ryu

NOG   035

182 Brick Lane, E1 6SA
020 7739 4134
www.noggallery.com
Tube: Liverpool Street
Open: Daily 12:00-18:00

This superlative little gallery/store/cafe specialises in alternative art and media. NOG (Nucleus of Observation & Graphics) stocks limited run books, 'zines, tees, vinyl and prints, and there is a cafe downstairs with exhibitions and live music.

no-one   036

1 Kingsland Road, E2 8AA
020 7613 5314
www.no-one.co.uk
Tube: Old Street or Liverpool Street
Open: Mon-Sat 11:00-19:00, Sunday 12:00-18:00

Teresa Letchford's no-one boutique is one of our favourite stores in town. A split space combining a licensed cafe/bar and fashion/lifestyle shop, the rails are bursting with the most exciting fashion talent in the world. Independent women's and menswear designers sit alongside collections from more established designers like Karen Walker, PPQ and Cheap Monday. Quirky gifts, accessories and

Rokit   037

101&107 Brick Lane, E1 6SE
020 7375 3864
www.rokit.co.uk
Tube: Liverpool Street
Open: Mon-Fri 11:00-19:00, Sat & Sun 10:00-19:00

Rokit launched its first store in Camden back in 1983, off the back of its stall on the Market. One of the first vintage outlets in London to present stock with an emphasis on the latest fashions, they soon attracted the attention of the style-hungry. Today, they continue their reign as leading retro retailers in the capital, with four stores dedicated to fashion from the 1940s onwards. Rokit offers a wide selection of unisex clothing, footwear and accessories, the quality of which guarantees them inclusion in the fashion pages of influential magazines. The smaller womenswear boutique (a few doors down) is more upmarket, stocking prettier styles with tulle skirts, furs, party dresses and evening shoes.

magazines bide for your attention while you sup a drink in the adjoining cafe. Letchford is making power moves on the Kingsland Road. Fast becoming the guvnor, she opened bar, DreamBagsJaguarShoes in 2002. She followed this with no-one — now a 'how-to' in fashion retail — and more recently, the Seventeen art gallery.

no-one photography by Keex

LIGHTSPEED CHAMPION

Q: WHICH VENUE DO YOU PREFER TO PLAY IN LONDON? *"The 100 Club, so many good people have played there. It's just a really cool place."*

Q: WHERE'S YOUR FAVOURITE PLACE TO EAT? *"The Diner on Curtain Road; I feel comforted there. I spent 4 hours there yesterday —— always the Cajun chicken burger and fries."*

Rough Trade photography by Keex featuring Lightspeed Champion in-store

Rough Trade East   038

Dray Walk (off Brick Lane), E1 6QL. T: 020 7392 7788. W: www.roughtrade.com
Tube: Liverpool Street. Open: Mon-Thu 08:00-22:00, Fri & Sat 08:00-20:00, Sun 11:00-19:00

No need for introductions here. London's most iconic independent record shop has been at the forefront of alternative music for over 30 years. While a relative newcomer to the capital's East End — all previous and existing shops being in the west — Rough Trade East could not be more at home in London's hipster-central. By far the largest store Rough Trade has ever opened, the cavernous 5000 sq ft space in Brick Lane's Old Truman Brewery also houses a cafe and an Internet-ready work area, as well as doubling as a live band space. Expect to find the latest underground music, all manner of music magazines, books and fanzines under one roof. An absolute must for discerning music fans and collectors.

Start   039

42-44 & 59 Rivington Street, EC2A 3BN. T: (W) 020 7729 3334; (M) 020 7739 3636
W: www.start-london.com. Tube: Liverpool Street. Open: Mon-Fri 10:30-18:30
Sat 11:00-18:00, Sun 13:00-17:00

ROUGH TRADE EAST — TOP LONDON SONGS

Lily Allen – *Ldn*
Squeeze – *Up The Junction*
Ldn is a Victim – *Ldn is a Victim*
The Clash – *White Riot*
The Pogues – *Misty Morning Albert Bridge*
Part Chimp – *New Cross*
Television Personalities – *Part Time Punks*
The Times – *Miss London*
Wendy James – *London's Brilliant*
The Jam – *Going Underground*
The Cockney Rejects – *I'm Forever Blowing Bubbles*
Carter USM – *Twenty Four Minutes From Tulse Hill*
Johnny Thunders – *London Boys*
Burial – *South London Boroughs*
Twisted Charm – *London Scene*

Fashion-meets-rock 'n' roll boutiques, Start womenswear and Start menswear are the brainchild of Philip Start and local rock darling, Brix Smith-Start (guitarist from The Fall). Both stores feature clothing and accessories from major and new designers worldwide including Nudie, Karen Walker, Miu Miu, Stella McCartney, See by Chloé and Comme des Garçons. The womenswear boutique has a shoe lounge with an additional section dedicated to sunglasses, bags, fragrance, and a skincare range from British company, REN. The two-floor Start menswear boasts an extensive jeans collection, the store's own label, Rivington Street, and a personal tailoring service. The founders have a keen eye for style and have created an aesthetic wonderland complete with boudoir-style changing rooms, art installations, and resident pug dog, Gromit.

Superette

66a Sclater Street, E1 6HR. T: 020 7033 4286. W: www.superette.co.uk Tube: Liverpool Street. Open: Mon-Fri 11:00-18:00, Sat & Sun 12:00-19:00

Superette is the retail equivalent of a candy cane being licked by a pop star at an all-night rave. Founded by the girls behind the lauded Lady Luck Rules OK rocker jewellery label, Superette is a quirky and dynamic studio-meets-retail space which serves as a blueprint for creativity. The girls make accessories out the back while you peruse rails of pretty dresses, crazy tees and sweats, marvelling at the sunglasses, badges, stationery, and overall gorgeousness of this shop.

Tatty Devine   041

236 Brick Lane, E2 7EB
020 7739 9191
www.tattydevine.com
Tube: Liverpool Street
Open: Daily 11:00-18:00

This brilliant little store houses the full collection of off-the-wall jewellery and accessories by the super-original British label, Tatty Devine. Despite its regular appearance in magazine fashion editorials, not to mention extensive stockists across the globe, somehow Tatty Devine has retained the independent, kooky attitude it had on launch. It's still a preferred label of girls who want their jewellery to make a bold statement, and it's also a great place to pick up lesser-known fashion designers.

The Three Threads   042

47-49 Charlotte Road, EC2A 3QT
020 7749 0503
www.thethreethreads.com
Tube: Old Street or Liverpool Street
Open: Mon-Sat 11:00-19:00, Sun 12:00-18:00

Stocking ultra-rare brands for men and women, The Three Threads boutique is a welcome breath of fresh air in an increasingly stagnated retail landscape. Steering clear of brand marketing hype and focusing exclusively on labels whose quality speaks for itself, the store carries a stellar list of streetwear brands including Japanese label, Tenderloin, artist Will Sweeney's Alakazam, the Sydney-based Supply label, Rittenhouse and NYC cult womenswear label, Built by Wendy, for which it is the only UK stockist. Label-related artists rotate their artwork in the space each season.

The Three Threads photography courtesy of The Three Threads
Tatty Devine photography by Keex

A Butcher of Distinction

11 Dray Walk, E1 6QL. T: 020 7770 6111
Tube: Liverpool Street. Open: Daily 10:00-19:00

A Butcher of Distinction brings you the latest in men's threads with collections by SILAS, Alife, Milkcrate Athletics, John Smedley, and One True Saxon.

Bad Bikes

107 Redchurch Street, E2 7DL. Tube: Bethnal Green or Liverpool Street. Open: Times vary

This quirky little vintage store specialises in all manner of paraphernalia from the 1980s to the early '90s. Rollerskates and racer bikes sell alongside Hi-Tec trainers, jelly shoes, shell suits and other signature styles from this era. The space itself has aspects of a teenager's bedroom complete with stacks of vinyl, accessory boxes displaying plastic and rubber jewellery and watches, and posters and retro lamps from back in the day.

Artwords Bookshop

65a Rivington Street, EC2A 3QQ. T: 020 7729 2000. W: www.artwords.co.uk. Tube: Liverpool Street or Old Street. Open: Mon-Sun 10:30-19:00

A tiny shop offering magazines and books covering art theory, graffiti, interior design, architecture and graphic design — many of which have been imported from around the world. Quality reads dominate the store so this is the place to pick up the rarer titles that you won't find on sale at the local newsagents.

Atlantis

7-9 Plumber's Row, E1 1EQ. T: 020 7377 8855 W: www.atlantisart.co.uk. Tube: Aldgate East or Liverpool Street. Open: Mon-Sat 09:00-18:00, Sun 10:00-17:00

Atlantis is a leading supplier of art materials in London. When local artists need product, this is where they shop. The store is set over several floors offering everything from canvases and papers to Montana spray paint, brushes, frames and books.

PHOTOGRAPHY

01 Concrete Hermit, Anthony Burrill exhibition;
photograph courtesy of Concrete Hermit
02 Luna and Curious photography by Keex

Beats Workin' Records

93-95 Sclater Street, E1 6HR. T: 020 7729 8249
W: www.beatsworkinrecords.com Tube: Liverpool
Street. Open: Tue-Sun 11:30-19:30

Flying the flag for smaller independent record shops in the area, Beats Workin' attracts crate-diggers and casual buyers alike. Covering a broad sweep of genres, it's a nicely stocked little spot, which is always worth a look. With reasonable prices and friendly staff, you should definitely check it out if you're in the area.

Behave

17 Lamb Street, E1 6EA. T: 020 7375 1617
Tube: Liverpool Street. Open: 11:00-19:00

The East End retail division of Soho boutique, Behave, introduces the most sought-after high-end denim and independent clothing labels from around the world, including Cheap Monday, Trainerspotter and APRIL77. This is a slimmed-down version of the original store, so if you want the full range of stock, head over to Soho – see page 76.

Blend

146 Bethnal Green Road, E2 6DG. T: 077 2089
0393. Tube: Bethnal Green or Liverpool Street
Open: Tue-Sun 11:00-19:00

Retro styling at its best, Blend carries a perfectly balanced stock of new and old streetwear. Highly edited product means the store carries no surplus crap. All of their very desirable vintage pieces are in excellent condition, but they still keep things affordable which is all too rare in retro boutiques these days. Blend also specialises in old school BMX and skate clothing and accessories, as well as graffiti products, including the full range of Montana spray paint.

Bodhi Gallery

214 Brick Lane, E1 6SA. T: 020 7749 0750
W: www.bodhigallery.tumblr.com Tube: Liverpool
Street. Open: Daily 11:00-00:00

A recent addition to Brick Lane's retail and cafe landscape, The Bohdi Gallery encompasses a cafe/sushi bar, contemporary art gallery and store selling vinyl toys, clothing, books and magazines. It's difficult to know where to begin with this one. Serving delicious Japanese food, the menu alone is reason to check this place out — seeing as it's the only place in the area to serve this cuisine. The gallery and retail space are also impressive. Essentially the same space as the cafe, surprisingly high-profile artists from around the world exhibit here, so you can enjoy your sushi, while taking in the artworks that surround you. It's a really interesting spot, and though multifaceted, which on paper sounds confusing, it actually works perfectly.

Bordello

55 Great Eastern Street, EC2A 3HP. W: www.bor-
dello-london.com Tube: Old Street. Open: Tue-Sat
11:30-19:00, Sun 12:00-17:30

The only lingerie and boudoir boutique in Shoreditch, Bordello has all your bedroom fashion and furniture requirements covered. Girls, if you're looking to incorporate some burlesque glamour into your lives, you'll find beautiful lingerie on sale here by a host of designers like Myla, Mimi Holiday, The Modern Courtesan, and Miss Katie. The emphasis is on the senses so whether you're looking for a sculpted couture corset, vintage and contemporary accessories or 18th century furniture, Bordello's got it all.

B&R London

128 Shoreditch High Street, E1 6JE. T: 020 7613
0606. Tube: Old Street. Open: Mon-Sat 10:00-
19:00, Sun 12:00-18:00

B&R London is a collaborative boutique by British fashion label, Religion Clothing, and new womenswear label, Bolongaro Trevor (by the founders of fashion brand, All Saints). Both labels have concessions elsewhere in London, but this is the only place to catch the full range.

Bread & Honey

205 Whitecross Street, EC1Y 8QP
T: 020 7253 4455. W: www.breadnhoney.com
Tube: Old Street. Open: Mon-Wed, Fri 10:00-
18:30, Thu 10:00-19:00, Sat 10:00-18:00

Excellent men and women's fashion boutique stocking labels like D.I.E, Futura, One True Saxon, Stüssy, Pointer, Laura Lees, and Kulte.

Brick Lane Market

Sclater Street/Brick Lane, E1 6QL. Tube: Liverpool Street. Open: Sun 08:00-15:00

Every Sunday morning, market traders set up stall here selling everything from clothing and knick-knacks to vinyl. Look out for locals who set up random collections of tat on the pavement.

Broadway Market

Broadway Market. T: 077 0931 1869. W: www.broadwaymarket.co.uk. Tube/Rail: London Fields rail or Hackney Central tube. Open: Sat 09:00-17:00

Arts and crafts, furniture, vinyl, vintage clothing, independent designers and food, every Saturday. There are numerous boutiques lining the market road including gallery/shop, Fabrications (no. 7 Broadway Market) which stocks a great selection of products hand-crafted by local designers.

Columbia Rd Flower Market

Columbia Road, 7NN. Tube: Old Street. Open: Sun 08:00-14:00

No visit to London is complete without a walk down Columbia Road Flower market on a Sunday morning. The market sells flowers and plants at wholesale prices (some traders reduce prices to £5 for three bunches after midday), so you can walk away with armfuls of domestic and exotic flowers for less than £20. Boutiques, delis and galleries line the street, particular favourites being cute cake shop, Treacle (no. 110-112), art print merchants, Nelly Duff (no. 156) and the vintage fashion stores including MadFashionBitch (no. 56). For lunch, head to Laxeiro (no. 93) for tapas or the Royal Oak (no. 73) for a Sunday roast — it's popular so you'll need to get here early or book ahead.

Concrete Hermit

5a Club Row, E1 6JX. T: 020 7729 2646 W: www.concretehermit.com Tube: Liverpool Street Open: Daily 10:00-18:00

This streetwear label works with illustrators-of-the-moment such as Kate Moross, to produce T-shirts, books, badges and more. They also host in-store art exhibitions.

F-Art

24 Cheshire Street, E2 6EH. T: 0 20 7729 5411 W: www.f-art.uk.com Tube: Liverpool Street Open: Sat 12:00-17:00, Sun 22:30-17:00

An independent art-centric design and gallery space which exhibits and sells new and vintage toys (including an authentic Keith Haring toy from his estate), graphic design books, rare copies of Interview magazine, ceramics, sculpture, furniture and more. F-Art also retails art prints.

The Laden Showroom

103 Brick Lane, E1 6SE. T: 020 7247 2431. W: www.laden.co.uk Tube: Liverpool Street. Open: Mon 12:00-18:00, Tue-Sat 11:00-18:30, Sun 10:30-18:00

Playing host to almost 50 independent designers, this Brick Lane store is crammed with unisex fashion and accessories at reasonable prices.

Luna and Curious

198 Brick Lane, E1 6SA. T: 020 7033 4411 W: www.lunaandcurious.com Tube: Liverpool Street

An exquisite range of vintage couture, rare jewellery, accessories and art.

Nelly Duff

156 Columbia Road, E2 7RG. T: 020 7613 4488 W: www.nellyduff.com Tube: Old Street or Bethnal Green. Open: Sat 14:00-18:00, Sun 09:00-15:00

Screen-print store specialising in urban art, illustration, design and graffiti. Artist works available include Shepard Fairey, Faile, Insect, Matthew Small, Mr Jago and Eine. Nelly Duff also hosts exhibitions every month.

Old Spitalfields Market

Commercial Street, E1 6BG
W: www.oldspitalfieldsmarket.com Tube: Liverpool
Street. Open: Thu-Fri 10:00-16:00, Sun 09:00-17:00

Massive indoor market selling crafts, independent fashion designs, vintage clothing, jewellery, assorted retro junk and organic food every Sunday. There is a fortnightly record fair housed here on Wednesdays which is a must-visit for vinyl aficionados.

Paper Dress

114-116 Curtain Road, EC2A 3AH
T: 020 7729 4100. W: www.paperdress.co.uk
Tube: Old Street or Liverpool Street. Open: Mon- Sat
11:30-19:30, Sun 13:00-18:00

Vintage clothing, footwear and accessories for men and women dating from the 1940s to the 1980s.

Public Beware Co

Shop 7, Dray Walk, E1 6QL. T: 020 7770 6213
Tube: Liverpool Street. Open: Mon-Thu, Sun 11:00-19:00, Fri & Sat 11:00-20:00

An excellent womenswear boutique selling independent designer clothing, footwear, accessories and second-hand vinyl. Public Beware stocks rare designers by the dozen, and with plenty of imports and cool labels, you never know what a hunt in this shop will turn up.

Ridley Road Market

Ridley Road, E8 2NP. T: 020 8356 3367
Rail: Dalston Kingsland. Open: Mon- Thu 06:00-18:00, Fri & Sat 06:00-19:00

Known locally as Dalston Market, this near-daily street market sells fruit, meat, fish and veg from around the world, in addition to clothing, fabric, household goods and various junk.

Sam Greenberg

64 Sclater Street, E1 6HR. T: 020 7033 4045
W: www.samgreenbergvintage.co.uk Tube: Liverpool
Street. Open: Tue-Fri 12:00-18:00, Sat & Sun 10:00-18:00

Soho's vintage clothing veterans offer a slice of their unisex retro fashion, footwear and accessories to east Londoners. This is the Sam Greenberg factory outlet so you're more likely to pick up a bargain here than in the Carnaby store.

Son of a Stag

9 Dray Walk, The Old Truman Brewery, E1 6QL
T: 020 7247 3333. Tube: Liverpool Street
Open: Daily 10:30-19:00

Streetwear store for men stocking British and international labels.

Sunday (UP) Market

Ely's Yard, Old Truman Brewery, E1 6QL
T: 020 7770 6028. W: www.sundayupmarket.co.uk
Tube: Liverpool Street. Open: Sun 10:00-17:00

Geared to a young crowd, this market hosts 140 stalls by up-and-coming fashion designers, jewellers and artists who gather every Sunday to sell their handprinted tees, homewares, bags, art and accessories. There are international food stalls, plus a decent selection of vintage clothes and shoes.

BEST FASHION STORES

b Store *page 74*

Beyond the Valley *page 76*

Concrete *page 77*

Dover Street Market *page 78*

Hoxton Boutique *page 36*

Kokon to Zai *page 82*

no-one *page 39*

TwoSee *page 91*

The Shop

3 Cheshire Street, E2 6ED. T: 020 7739 5631
Tube: Liverpool Street. Open: Mon-Sat 11:00-18:00
Sun 11:00-16:30

This tiny vintage boutique is a bit like shopping in someone's wardrobe. Although the fashion and shoe sections are limited, it stocks some quality vintage garments, fabrics and accessories for men and women.

This Shop Rocks

131 Brick Lane, E1 6SE. T: 020 7739 7667
Tube: Liverpool Street. Open: Daily 12:00-19:00

This Brick Lane boutique sells vintage clothing and accessories along with customised garments and one-off creations.

D*FACE ARTIST

Q: What's your favourite London store? "Gloria's on Dray Walk." Q: Where's your favourite drinking haunt in London StolenSpace openings. The drink's free and the work always on point!" Q: What's the funniest thing you have seen happening at an art exhibition? "So many things that have made me laugh it's hard to pull up one. I recently got back from a museum show in Germany (I normally roll with my boy Word to Mother to help set up and lend a hand); well, I exhibited an upside down cross made up of multiple brand logos. The cross stood about 10ft tall. The museum was a converted church, so it fitted perfectly and I knew it would be met with a mixed reaction. Someone talking to Word to Mother thought he was the artist and asked what it meant. He politely explained that it was essentially what we've come to worship; that the crucifix itself was a strange 'mark' to use as a sign of worship as it represents torture, and that this piece represented the combination of the two. She, disgusted with the use of the cross, said 'Oh, and you'd do this in a church in London would you?' in a very demeaning manner. His reply was so classic Brit abroad: 'Luv, we do whatever the fuck

EAST ART

Black Rat Press; photography by Ian Cox

Guerilla art exhibitions pop up all over London, so keep an eye out on the latest temporary shows by visiting www.pimpguides.com where you'll find up-to-the-minute art news. The Old Truman Brewery around Brick Lane often hosts one-off art shows, and the Village Underground—a space with disused tube train carriages suspended over the roof — is a popular choice for exhibitors at 54 Holywell Lane, Shoreditch, EC2A 3PQ

Black Rat Press   043

Arch 461, 83 Rivington Street, EC2A 3AY
T: 020 7613 7200
W: www.blackratpress.co.uk
Tube: Liverpool Street or Old Street
Open: Tue, Wed & Fri 10:00-18:00, Thu 10:00-21:00, Sat 10:00-16:00

Black Rat Press regularly curates solo and group exhibitions at their new East End gallery, accessed via the back of Cargo's yard. Playing host to an ever-expanding roster of world-leading graffiti artists including Swoon, D*Face, Blek le Rat and Nick Walker, this gallery is one to watch.

Leonard Street *Gallery*   044   Seventeen   045

73A Leonard Street, EC2A 4QS
020 7033 9977
www.tlsg.co.uk
Tube: Old Street
Open: Mon-Fri 11:00-18:00, Sat 11:00-15:00

17 Kingsland Road, E2 8AA
020 7729 5777
www.seventeengallery.com
Tube: Old Street or Liverpool Street
Open: Wed-Sat 11:00-18:00

The Leonard Street Gallery is one of the most exciting art galleries to launch in London in recent years. Featuring the biggest names in the industry, the gallery programme reads like a who's-who of contemporary and street art. Artists who've exhibited here include such luminaries as Banksy, Barry McGee, Faile, Blek le Rat, Nick Walker, D*Face, Jeff Soto, Swoon, Eine and Herakut. Admission to the gallery is free of charge.

For image, see page 50

Seventeen gallery (brought to us by the duo behind DreamBagsJaguarShoes and no-one boutique) plays host to burgeoning talent in contemporary and underground art. Exhibitors to date include the subversive art collective, CutUp whose reworkings of billboards and bus stop signs have led to some of the best campaigns since Dr D and AdBusters. You can expect a diverse roster of artists on show here, many of whom have influences rooted in pop culture.

CutUp Machine, 2005 Exhibition; photography by Dave Hoyland, courtesy of Seventeen

01-03 CHRIS LEVINE
'Lightness of Being'; photography
by Mark Whitfield at www.mark-
whitfieldphotography.com

04-05 WORD TO MOTHER
*'Dead Trees, Yellow Leaves, Cups
of Tea'*; photograph by
www.fatsarazzi.co.uk
courtesy of StolenSpace

StolenSpace

Off Dray Walk, E1 6QL
020 7247 2684
www.stolenspace.com
Tube: Liverpool Street
Open: Wed-Sun 11:00-19:00

When street artist, D*Face first arrived in the Big Smoke back in 1999, he rapidly established his reputation across London and the rest of the globe for his striking public artworks. In 2004, he became a gallery owner, setting up the Outside Institute — a showcase of the best in street art. The inaugural show gave SEEN, the Godfather of Graffiti, his first ever UK exhibition. This was followed by a wealth of other street artists, old and new, including Banksy, Blade, Zedz, Tracy 168, Dave the Chimp and Flying Förtress. Now running under a new name, StolenSpace, in the East End, the gallery has established itself as the area's finest. It recently played host to Shepard Fairey's *'NINETEENEIGHTY-FOURIA'* exhibition, and houses a permanent collection of artwork by Conor Harrington, Hellovon, Dave Kinsey, D*Face and Dan Witz. New exhibitions open on a monthly basis and it's the best place in London to catch legendary artists with a background in skateboard graphics, graffiti, illustration, comic book and tattoo art. If you only make it to one art gallery in east London, make it this one.

EINE
/ Graffiti Artist /

Q: SOMEONE ARRIVES IN LONDON. WHERE DO YOU TAKE THEM? *"I would take them to Columbia Road Flower Market, and then for a Sunday roast in the Bistrotheque."*

EINE 'Vandalism'; photograph courtesy of Eine

Pure Evil Gallery

108 Leonard Street, EC2A 4RH. T: 07805 420771. W: www.pureevilclothing.com Tube: Old Street. Open: Daily 10:00-18:00

Run by local artist, PURE EVIL, this Shoreditch gallery is a mecca for global street art. Exhibiting lesser-known artists, the gallery's ethos is to focus on more obscure, peripheral talent from around the world, to bring exposure to artists who wouldn't necessarily receive it. A visit here is educational as much as it is enjoyable. A great way to discover new art, Pure Evil is way ahead of the curve in this respect. Recommended, obviously.

The Aquarium L-13

63 Farringdon Road, EC1M 3JB. T: 020 3206 0008. W: www.theaquariumon-line.co.uk Tube: Farringdon. Open: Mon- Sat 11:00-18:00

An independent art gallery and store specialising in reactionary artists including punk's most famous situationist, Jamie Reid. Renowned for his work with the Sex Pistols, Jamie's latest and oldest works are housed at the Aquarium along with pieces by artists such as Billy Childish, Anne Pigalle and The KLF's James Cauty, who hit the headlines when he burned one-million quid. At the store, you can buy tees, music and artwork.

Art Vinyl Gallery

20 Broadway Market, E8 4PH. T: 020 72414129. www.artvinyl.com Tube: Bethnal Green Open: Thu-Sun 11:00-18:00

A groundbreaking gallery on Broadway Market exclusively dedicated to vinyl cover art. DJs associated with the art are often found playing here on Saturdays. Curators change every fortnight ensuring a steady stream of fresh exhibits.

The Barbican Centre

Silk Street, EC2Y 8DS. T: 020 7638 8891. W: www.barbican.org.uk Tube: Barbican. Open: Mon-Sat 09:00-23:00, Sun 12:00-23:00

The City of London houses what Her Majesty has described as 'one of the wonders of the modern world'. Debatable, but The Barbican is no doubt an impressive centre for contemporary art, music and film. The venue umbrellas an art gallery (past shows include David LaChapelle's photography exhibition); a music hall that invites world, jazz and classical acts to its stage, and three cinemas which project a reel of indie, arthouse and the odd Hollywood blockbuster. Film festivals, director Q&As and screen-talks run throughout the year.

stolenspace GALLERY

The Old Truman Brewery 91 Brick Lane London E1 6QL
T:020 7247 2684 E:info@stolenspace.com

OPENING TIMES: TUESDAY TO SUNDAY 10.30AM - 7PM

stolenspace.com

STREET ART

You'll find the better street art in London's East End. Some walls, such as that of Cargo (page 16), host permanent works by **Banksy** plus temporary works by majors like **Shepherd Fairey, Faile and Nick Walker**. Also keep your eyes peeled for billboards in this neighbourhood, which have been known to have their ad slogans subverted with humorous and often politically-loaded messages by **Dr D.**

For interviews with the leading street artists worldwide, plus images of their latest works, visit **www.pimpguides.com**

FORSTER Gallery

1 Chapel Place, Rivington Street, EC2A 3DQ. T: 020 7739 7572. W: www.forstergallery.com Tube: Old Street. Open: Wed-Fri 12:00-18:00, Sat 12:00-17:30

Launched in 2007, FORSTER deals in eminent names in contemporary and urban art including the infamous British freestyle graffiti artist, Xenz. See interview, page 102

XENZ 'Two in the Bush' photograph courtesy of Xenz at www.xenz.org. Artwork © Xenz, 2008

Kemistry Gallery

43 Charlotte Road, EC2A 3PD. T: 020 7749 2766 W: www.kemistrygallery.co.uk Tube: Old Street. Open: Mon-Fri 09:30-18:00, Sat 11:00-16:00

Kemistry focuses on contemporary and underground art, with shows by artists and collectives such as Eine and CutUp.

Modern Art

10 Vyner Street, E2 9DG. T: 020 8980 7742. Tube: Bethnal Green. Open: Thu-Sun 11:00-18:00 and by appointment

Behind this steel door in Bethnal Green lies a nice art space which exhibits a global mix of contemporary artists. Past artists have included San Francisco native, Barry McGee (Twist); Nigel Cooke; and Californian artist and pro-skateboarder, Ed Templeton, whose storming first UK solo show, 'The Judas Goat' gave Londoners a glimpse into US West Coast counter-culture.

MOT International

54 Regents Studios, 8 Andrews Road, E8 4QN. T: 020 7923 9561. W: www.mot-international.org Tube: Bethnal Green. Open: Thu-Sun 12:00-18:00

An independent artist-run exhibition space which has show-cased the work of over 150 artists since its inception, most notably Jake & Dinos Chapman.

Pure Evil Gallery

See the gallery featured opposite.

Signal Gallery

96a Curtain Road, EC2A 3AA. T: 020 7613 1550. W: www.signalgallery.com Tube: Old Street. Open: Tue-Sat 12:00-18:00 and by appointment

A contemporary art gallery in Hoxton featuring artists who work in figuration.

Strychnin Gallery

65 Hanbury Street, E1 5JP. W: www.strychnin.com. Tube: Liverpool Street Open: Fri-Sun 12:00-18:00

This is Strychnin Gallery's latest offering, adding to a gallery portfolio which now encompasses London, Berlin and New York. Curator, Yasha Young presents artists from all over the world who have a background in lowbrow dark art. A welcome addition to east London's celebrated art scene.

Whitechapel Art Gallery

Angel Alley Entrance, 80-82 Whitechapel High Street, E1 7QX. T: 020 7522 7888 W: www.whitechapel.org Tube: Aldgate East. Open: Mon-Fri 11:00-18:00

The soul of the East End community, the renowned 100-year-old Whitechapel Art Gallery specialises in international modern and contemporary art, offering a regular programme of exhibitions, films, talks, poetry, events, and live music.

White Cube

48 Hoxton Square, N1 6PB. T: 020 7930 5373. W: www.whitecube.com Tube: Old Street. Open: Tue-Sat 10:00-18:00

Jay Jopling's acclaimed gallery on Hoxton Square presents solo and group shows featuring today's most important contemporary artists including Tracey Emin, Lucian Freud, Gilbert & George, Chuck Close and Damien Hirst.

Namalee

Singer/Songwriter/Co-Founder of SuperSuper

Photography by Simian Coates

Q: Someone arrives in London for 4 hours. Where do you take them? "I would take them straight to central London and waltz down Oxford Street with them. We could rollerskate down the centre of the street, maybe hanging onto the back of a London bus. We'd go to all the cheap tat shops and buy a million hats, trashy lingerie, some 'I heart London' tee shirts and £1 jewellery. Then we would go for a ride on the London Eye and then we could pop in to SuperSuper Towers in Tin Pan Alley and they could partake in one of our morning raves. If we had time, we could go to Trafalgar Square and sunbathe with the pigeons too." **Q: Where's your first stop when shopping for clothes?** "Kokon To Zai — it's still amazing and their Noki Darkhorse collaborations are always sold out in a matter of days. I'm obsessed with Noki so I go straight there." **Q: Favourite club nights?** "Ah so many: Nuke 'em All run by BBoss is brilliant; For3ign; Wet Yourself; Chockablock; Dirty Canvas, and Niyi is starting a new club soon and I'm sure that will become my new favourite!" **Q: Which areas represent the city's richest fashion veins?** "Shoreditch is still the most fashion conscious area, but I also like to hang out with the tourists and admire their backpacks in Leicester Square." **Q: Where's your favourite drinking haunt?** "Ed's Diner on Old Compton street, for peanut butter and banana milkshake." **Q: The best London fashion designer at present is...** "Basso and Brooke — they are in a league of their own. They've started doing homeware and are about to launch their first perfume. Power print technicolour heaven!" **Q: What distinguishes London from every other city in the world?** "It's cold, grey, unkempt and way expensive but London has an incredible unique and vibrant buzz that I have never felt anywhere else in the world ever. I LOVE London — multiculti centre of the looniverse."

Central

Shop till you drop. It's what we all aspire to do. But, there's no romance without finance, especially when the object of your desire is a new pair of heels. We've all done the **Covent Garden** crawl or the **Soho** shuffle, but these aren't dance steps you can learn in any class. Whether getting bright and brash in **Soho's Kokon to Zai** or waiting for the latest sneaker drop outside Foot Patrol, the term 'money talks and bullshit walks' has never been so relevant. But, central London is not all about overdrafts and maxed-out cards. Circus is the celebrity club night that sets up the surreal scene of members of **Girls Aloud DJing** to a room full of **club-kids** while a glamorous cross-dresser called **Jodie Harsh** hosts. Quaff your champagne and throw your Topshop jewellery in the sky while you dance to electro and comment on that boy's fabulously silver shoes. Go on, you know you want to. But first you've got to get your outfit right. Elephantine celebrations of excess like Selfridges and Harrods may make you dizzy, but those **Westwood** stilettos are a must. And you can't leave without buying that belt. Hit the streets and arrogant tourists try to walk straight through you, but they know no better, so fuck 'em. You got your nails done and your hair did. It's back to Soho to slide down to the essential weekly hangout, **Punk.** Or you could drop into an **overpriced club** to play 'spot the Z-list celeb' and shake a leg to some funky house. The choice is yours.

SuperSuper party at PUNK, see page 70, photography by Billa

Drinking in central London can be amazingly good fun. However, on arrival, it can appear there's little more than drab chain bars and tourist pubs on offer. You need to scratch the surface, be proactive; the good stuff always needs to be hunted, that's what makes new cities so exciting. And so in the spirit of adventure, we've gone and done the scratching for you, compiling a list of the best bars and clubs in the centre, to save you those frustrating hours spent

100 Club   001

100 Oxford Street, W1D 1LL
020 7636 0933
www.the100club.co.uk
Tube: Tottenham Court Road
Open: Times vary

Since 1942, the 100 Club has been a vital venue on London's celebrated live music scene. The site of legendary performances by the Sex Pistols, the Rolling Stones, The White Stripes and The Clash, this place previews the stars of tomorrow with live bands most nights of the week. An intimate venue with a history deserving of its own book, the 100 Club will continue to break new bands and host many an illustrious gig to come.

Bloomsbury Bowling Lanes   002

Basement of Tavistock Hotel, Bedford Way, WC1H 9EU
020 7183 1979
www.bloomsburybowling.com
Tube: Russell Square
Open: Mon-Thu 12:00–02:00, Fri & Sat 12:00–03:00, Sun 13:00–00:00

The Bloomsbury Bowling Lanes is a hybrid entertainment venue offering 10-pin bowling, cinema, private karaoke, DJ bar, restaurant and live music. The 1950s-styled establishment attracts a varied clientele and its one of the few places in London where indie kids rub shoulders with West End after-work crowds. Nestled in the basement of the Tavistock Hotel, the Bloomsbury Bowling Lanes offers an alternative night out, and for several nights a week, a chance to catch up-and-coming bands. DJs like Rob da Bank can be found playing in the bar, independent film companies screen in the cinema, and the venue is often used for record label launches, video shoots and rockabilly club nights.

Jodie Harsh

Q: Someone arrives in London for only 4 hours and you are their guide. Where do you take them? "I love to shop, and I especially love to shop for clothes. There's a boutique in Soho called Kokon to Zai which is something of a mecca for the fashionista-hipsters of Shoreditch — I know a few who make a commute on the Northern line from East to West End on a weekly basis to check out their latest stock deliveries. Kokon is part owned by designer Marjan Pejovski, who created the swan dress that Björk wore to The Oscars. As well as clothes, they also have a great selection of vinyl and arty magazines. After we're shopped out, we'd head to Hoxton to check out whatever is showing at the White Cube gallery. If we're in luck it might be Sam Taylor-Wood or Tracey Emin. We'd grab a burger at Bar Music Hall, a restaurant which transforms into a club at night, to line our stomachs. Finally, if it's a Friday, we'd hit Circus at Soho Revue Bar to dance the night away."

DJ/Promoter/Socialite, Jodie Harsh runs club night, FOR3IGN!! at Bar Music Hall every Saturday night, along with performance artist, Scottee. See page 14. Jodie Harsh photography by Billa

003

The End

8 West Central Street, WC1A 1JJ
020 7419 9199
www.endclub.com
Tube: Tottenham Court Road
Open: Times vary. Typically open Fri 22.00-06.00, Sat 22:00-08:00
(DURRR is open Mon 22:30-03.00)

Undoubtedly the best club in central London for underground dance music, The End hosts some of the capital's finest nights. The best-dressed club kids from all over town pour into The End every Monday night for DURRR — a showcase of the most exciting new music with performances by live acts and DJs like Justice, Foals, Busy P, Erol Alkan and Skull Juice. DJs from around the globe display their skills across two rooms with a sound system that packs the punch needed to create an electric atmosphere. They say that music is in the blood, well here it could be said that the music flows thick and deep in its walls. The End is owned by legendary DJ/producer Mr C, who has brought the fundamentals of DJing into the club, from its constant stream of first-rate acts, eclectic music policy and sound quality, to the atmosphere and energy. It's a simple mix but one overlooked by so many music venues. Whether you visit on a Monday or a Friday, every night has a weekend vibe.

DURRR at The End; photography by Billa

ALI LOVE

Q: Someone arrives in London for only 4 hours and you are their guide. Where do you take them? "It depends. If it was a fit girl, I'd take her home and knock her up for a few hours. If it was a guy, I'd take him to the pub. I am a Neanderthal!"

The **Endurance** 004

90 Berwick Street, W1F 0QB
020 7437 2944
Tube: Oxford Circus or Tottenham Court Road
Open: Mon-Wed 12:30-23:00, Thu-Sat 12:30-23.30
Sun 13:00-17:00

Located in the heart of Soho, this old market pub is a wa-
tering hole for all the local characters who work in the
area. Attracting both scorn and praise in equal measure,
it is filled with vacuous media-types and pseudo-
celebrities most days of the week, and you'll be privy to
some jaw-dropping, laugh-out-loud examples of self-im-
portance. But, you won't find a livelier pub in the area.
The best time to go (in our opinion) is in the afternoon,
when after a hard day's shopping, you can have a pint
and grab a bite to eat. One of the pub's main draws is the
little beer garden out back, which is packed during the
summer months, when this place comes into its own.

Madame JoJo's 005

10 Brewer Street, London W1F 0SE
020 7734 3040
www.madamejojos.com
Tube: Piccadilly Circus
Open: (White Heat: Tue 20:00-03.00 / Deep Funk: Fri 10:00-03:00 / Lost &
Found: Sat 22:00-03:00)

Nestled in the bosom of sex sodden Soho, Madame JoJo's is
a sanctuary for those seeking solace from the soulless bars
which have so infected London. Clothed in red and velvet,
JoJo's former days as a transvestite cabaret club hang thick
in the air and this old world glamour makes it the perfect
venue for Keb Darge's Legendary Deep Funk, rockabilly
party, Lost & Found, and Tuesday night indie-rock club,
White Heat, where artists like The Horrors, Bloc Party and
Lethal Bizzle feature alongside the label's own signings.
London's young music cognoscenti turn out en mass for this
night such is its status for previewing quality music.

Mahiki 006

1 Dover Street, W1S 4LD
020 7493 9529
www.mahiki.com
Tube: Green Park
Open: Mon-Sat 17:30-03:30

This tiki cocktail club is an upmarket establishment most of
the time, but come Tuesday, residents ArtArtArt arrive and
the party gets underway. Hosted by the team behind Smash
& Grab (see page 71), ArtArtArt offers the latest sounds, art
and dress-up madness against a backdrop of Polynesian stat-
ues, leaf-effect banquettes and cushions. Ushering in the
young from around London, this gig introduces special con-
cepts each week such as live body painting by Kate Moross
and live music and DJing from artists like Plastic Little. You
can even star in your own music video in The Popbox.

Metro 007

9-23 Oxford Street, W1D 2DN
020 7437 0964
www.blowupmetro.com
Tube: Tottenham Court Road
Open: Times vary

Metro is a live music spot, made famous by the wealth
of bands and artists who have cut their teeth here.
Despite its small size and and no-frills interior, Metro
is a great little club, its history cemented by The White
Stripes dropping in to catch a gig here. An anything-
goes music policy saw The Libertines once play an
impromptu set, and Metro has also seen early shows by
Kings of Leon, Klaxons and Chromeo. With live performances most nights of the week, it's an essential gig
venue for anyone interested in music.

The Teenagers at PUNK; photography by Billa

THE TEENAGERS

DORIAN (Guitarist)

Q: *Where's your favourite place to go drinking?* "I like to go to Durrr on Monday at The End, and sometimes in Shoreditch: The Old Blue Last or Electricity Showrooms." Q: *What distinguishes London from every other city in the world?* "Everyone is crazy for parties here. It's always good fun everywhere, and every day of the week you can have fun. It's not like that at all in Paris. And people are so into it; it's unbelievable for a French person at first sight."

PUNK

008

14 Soho Street, W1D 3DN
020 7734 4004
www.punksoho.com
Tube: Tottenham Court Road
Open: Mon-Fri 17:00-03:00, Sat 21:00-03:00

PUNK is the current club of choice for London's scenester and celebrity set with Kate Moss and Kelly Osborne regularly hitting the Queens of Noize's weekly Smash & Grab party. With live music sets, art exhibitions and club nights presented by current scene-stars like NIYI, you're guaranteed some of the most upfront parties in London. In terms of clubs that attract the music, fashion and arty crowd, you won't find better in the West End. IHEARTNIYI is at Punk every Tuesday night. Smash & Grab is every Thursday.

SOHO REVUE BAR

11 Walkers Court, Brewer Street, W1F OED. T: 020 7734 0377
W: www.sohorevuebar.com Tube: Piccadilly Circus. Open: Tue-Sun 20:00-04:00

Every Friday night within the glamorous environs of the Soho Revue Bar, Jodie Harsh brings club kids and celebrities together for the weekly extravaganza, Circus. Here, the most influential heads in fashion and music fill the chandelier-lit dance floor and party alongside circus performers and London's flamboyant youth. A decadent playground, Circus welcomes everyone from Gareth Pugh and Amanda Lepore to its stage, while celebrities take to the decks, playing a mix of electro, disco and indie-pop.

ULU

010

Malet Street, WC1E 7HY. T: 020 7664 2000
W: www.barflyclub.com/ulu Tube: Goodge Street. Open: Times vary
Doors are usually 19:00-23:00

The ULU is a university-based live music venue which plays host to up-and-coming bands. For over 50 years, rising stars have been performing here, with gigs by an alumnus of artists including The Strokes, Pink Floyd and Babyshambles. It's not just students who visit ULU; the venue attracts a mixed crowd of music fans and industry types, keen to catch the best new sounds. Its university location also means you'll enjoy cheap drink.

ASTORIA

157 Charing Cross Road, WC2 8EN. T: 020 7434 9592
W: www.festivalrepublic.com Tube: Tottenham Court Road. Open: Times vary

A chewing gum spit from Centre Point, the Astoria is one of London's most famous live music venues. Made legendary by performances from the Rolling Stones, David Bowie and Prince, the theatre is still a regular performance spot for major acts like the Gossip and Kings of Leon, along with bands about to blow up.

Astoria 2

165 Charing Cross Road, WC2 0EN. T: 020 7434 9592
W: www.festivalrepublic.com Tube: Tottenham Court Road. Open: Times vary

Named the Astoria 2 in respect to its larger neighbouring sibling, this 1000-capacity venue introduces quality bands, new and old. Once through the mirrored stairwell, you have access to two levels so you can enjoy gigs either down and dirty in the pit or above the madness on the oversized balcony, where the likelihood of losing half your pint is greatly reduced. Much like the Astoria, it attracts world-famous acts and has seen performances by Iggy Pop, Primal Scream, and many more.

BLOOMSBURY BALLROOM

Victoria House, 37-63 Bloomsbury Square, WC1B 4DA. T: 020 7404 7612
W: www.bloomsburyballroom.co.uk Tube: Russell Square. Open: Times vary

London's embrace of art deco glamour continues apace, reaching its zenith with the salubrious stylings of this stunning new venue. The space boasts an elegant ballroom and stage, and can also be transformed into an 800-capacity live concert hall.

The Borderline

Orange Yard (off Manette Street), W1D 4JB. T: 020 7734 5547
W: www.meanfiddler.com Tube: Tottenham Court Road. Open: Times vary

A tiny basement venue, a tad shabby, but with a relaxed, block-party atmosphere concealed down a conveniently-central back alley. Regularly showcasing new bands (and hosting secret gigs), The Borderline is also known for its midweek indie/alternative club nights, where piles of youth litter the stage area, and Snakebite is downed with venom.

Bradley's Spanish Bar

42-44 Hanway Street, W1T 1UP. T: 020 7636 0359. Tube: Tottenham Court Road
Open: Mon-Sat 12:00-23:00, Sun 15:00-22:30

Tucked away off Oxford Street, this tiny pub is a great find, and a convenient refreshment stop-off when shopping in the area. The street level bar (with a max capacity of about 20), is warm, cosy and inviting. If you can't find a perching space, venture down the Lilliputian stairwell to the basement, squeeze into an alcove and soak up the atmosphere. The perfect soundtrack is provided by an old school jukebox, blaring out dusty 45s. BTW, the only Spanish reference that comes to mind is the San Miguel on tap.

Ghetto

5-6 Falconberg Court, W1D 3AB. T: 0207 287 3726
W:www.ghetto-london.co.uk Tube: Tottenham Court Road. Open: Times vary

Ghetto is probably most famous for Friday's notorious gay night, The Cock (hosted by Princess Julia — co-founder of music 'zine, *The Pix*), and midweek gig, NagNagNag. Predominantly a gay club, this dark and sweaty venue is usually packed with a crowd of cross-dressers, club kids of an electro and indie-pop persuasion, and tourists who have stumbled in here unwittingly given its central location.

THE JOHN SNOW

39 Broadwick Street, w1f 9qj. T: 020 7437 1344. Tube: Oxford Circus
Open: Mon-Sat: 12:00-23:00, Sun 12:00-22:30

Named after the doctor who discovered cholera was a waterborne disease (from a water pump that once stood on the same site), The John Snow is the area's most authentic Victorian pub. So damn charming, it is packed with period features and can't have looked much different in its heyday. If you're not one for bars pretending to be pubs and want a proper Soho boozer, this is the place for you. Also, it's a Samuel Smiths Pub (a brewery, for those who don't know), which means cheap drinks.

The Social

5 Little Portland Street, W1W 7JB. T: 020 7636 4992. W: www.thesocial.com
Tube: Oxford Circus. Open: Mon-Wed 12:00-00:00, Thu-Sat 12:00-01:00

For years now, Heavenly Recordings' The Social has been an industrial little oasis in the desert that is central London's bar scene. Within the venue's particularly distinctive layout, DJs consistently supply quality music to a varied crowd of after-work suits, media types and students.

SIN

144 Charing Cross Road, WC2H 0LB. T: 020 7240 1900
W:www.sinlondon.com Tube: Tottenham Court Road. Open: Times vary

A decadent Soho club playing host to alternative gigs including Friday night gay residency, Popstarz. With Fore3gn DJs dropping by spinning a mix of electro, disco and new rave, the opulent multiple-room venue is transformed into a playground, complete with a Pop Lounge and Rave Room.

For the uninitiated, shopping in central London can be a nightmare. If you're not accustomed to its labyrinthine network of streets, successfully navigating a path in search of those hidden boutiques and exclusive stores can be tricky to say the least. The cobbled backstreets and laneways that make up much of the city's shopping districts, while charming in a Dickensian sort of a way, can prove very confusing. Swallowing up the lost is what this city does best. Even for the weathered global-shopper with a sense of direction honed in cities like New York or Tokyo, London's serpentine layout presents a uniquely challenging retail landscape. It's what makes exploring and discovering its hidden retail gems so rewarding. Even so, we know no one's above a little heads-up on where's good and how to get there, so here we assist you in getting straight to the best stuff.

6 Newburgh Street
011

6 Newburgh Street, W1 7RQ
020 7734 9976
www.adidas.com
Tube: Oxford Circus
Open: Mon-Sat 10:30-18:30, Sun 13:00-17:00

Showcasing the legendary three-stripe mega brand, this sleek Adidas concept boutique off Carnaby Street acts more like a gallery than an actual retail store. Exclusive releases including footwear, jackets, tees and other limited edition apparel, perch and pose at angles, and while many pieces are available to purchase, ultimately the public is teased with a small glimpse of the jewels. No. 6 receives first deliveries of exclusive edition launches, encouraging the hunter/gatherer state of mind in dedicated heads. For the flagship, head over to Adidas Originals in Covent Garden where all exhibits are available to purchase, and stock relies on the quirkier aspects of the Adidas collection, with unique colourways and cuts for both male and female aficionados.

ADIDAS ORIGINALS: 9 Earlham Street, WC2H 9LL. T: 020 7379 4042
Tube: Covent Garden. Open: Mon-Sat 10:30-19:00, Sun 13:00-17:00

B STORE
012

24a Savile Row, W1S 3PR
020 7734 6846
www.bstorelondon.com
Tube: Oxford Circus
Open: Mon-Fri 10:30-18.30, Sat 10:00-18:00

Rightfully describing itself as 'a mecca for new fashion talent', the award-winning b Store is a beacon of style with an unparalleled choice of niche collections, and up-and-coming and graduate fashion designers. Established in 2000, b Store caters to London's tastemakers. Immaculately presented, the Savile Row store stocks collections from Peter Jensen, Siv Støldal, Cosmic Wonder, Bless, Ute Ploier, Bernhard Willhelm, Luke Hall and Stephan Schneider, as well as its own range of beautifully-crafted footwear. Perhaps the biggest coup of all is the helpful and friendly owners and staff who have managed all this without a hint of pretension or elitism.

Q: Where's your first stop when shopping for clothes? "I love the boutique-style shops that London has such as Hoxton Boutique, b Store, Beyond the Valley & Start. The boutiques in Shoreditch and on Conduit Street are to me London's greatest fashion stores. For vintage, the big warehouse place on Holloway Road. For high-end/designer, I love Dover Street Market, and Selfridges is always great for a one-stop shop."

STYLIST / DESIGNER **nova**

BAPE

4 Upper James Street, W1F 9DG   013
020 7494 4924
www.bape.com
Tube: Piccadilly Circus
Open: Mon-Fri 11:00-19:00, Sat 11:00-18:00

Although the once uber-rare Japanese clothing label, A Bathing Ape has now become a staple on the backs and feet of hip hop artists and pop stars the world over, what many don't know is that the first store to open outside of Asia was actually in London, back in 2002. Way before the alleged 'style icons' Pharrell Williams and Kanye West could even find Japan on a map, switched-on Londoners have been rocking A Bathing Ape. There is a good reason owner, Nigo chose to open his first store in London and not New York people, but I suppose you knew that, because you're here.

BEYOND the VALLEY   015

2 Newburgh Street, W1F 7RD
020 7437 7338
www.beyondthevalley.com
Tube: Oxford Circus
Open: Mon-Sat 11:00-18:30, Sun 12:30-17:00

Beyond the Valley stocks over 100 fashion labels, artists and designer/makers over two floors in this excellent Soho boutique. A creative enterprise founded by three fashion graduates, the store acts as a test platform offering support to emerging talent. Beyond the Valley features limited-run collections by graduates of London's most prestigious fashion, art and design colleges, with many labels exclusive to the store. You'll find rare and innovative product here, reflecting the more exciting and experimental design that comes out of the capital. Clothing, jewellery, homeware, artwork and accessories are all on offer in this small and kooky space. The store also boasts a gallery which plays host to a regular programme of art exhibitions.

Beyond the Valley photography by Naughty James

BEHAVE

48 Lexington Street, W1F 0LR   014
020 7734 6876
Tube: Oxford Circus
Open: Daily 11:00-19:00

Behave's small yet perfectly formed boutiques are a one-stop shop for the growing number of high-end denim and independent clothing labels to emerge from around the world in recent years. Alongside the popular Ksubi (formerly Tsubi), labels such as Minimarket, Carin Webster and Cheap Monday can be found in-store, as well as a number of select brands including French jeans label, APRIL77, Trainerspotter and Umbro by Kim Jones. This is a store with a nice range of alternative product not widely available in the UK. If you're making a trip to the East End, you'll find BEHAVE's newest store in Spitalfields: 17 Lamb Street, E1 6EA. T: 020 7375 1617. Tube: Liverpool Street.

BLACK PEARL

Black Pearl photography by Keex

Unit 2.10 Kingly Court, W1B 5PW
020 7439 0702
www.blackpearlboutique.co.uk
Tube: Oxford Circus
Open: Mon-Sat 11:00-19:00, Sun 12:00-18:00

016

Fiona Deffenbaugh introduces an original collection of retro Vegas-influenced jewellery in this 1950s tiki-style boutique. In addition to selling her own magnificent Def Design jewellery, Fiona sources independent designer and vintage clothing, lingerie, corsets and handmade accessories which are inspired by mods & rockers and glamour pin-ups like Bettie Page. If you like this style and are seeking some unique labels and accessories, the Black Pearl boutique is for you.

Browns comprises five outlets across London, each showcasing a highly-edited selection of the world's leading designers. The South Molton Street stores stock collections by 140+ designers including Stella McCartney, Matthew Williamson and Marc Jacobs. Browns Focus is the best of the stable, geared towards the more cutting edge market who seek up-and-coming labels and plenty of international imports. This is a regular destination of those with money to burn and a passion for the latest, exclusive collections.

Browns Focus

017

38-39 South Molton Street, W1K 5RN
020 7514 0063
www.brownsfashion.com
Tube: Bond Street
Open: Mon, Wed, Fri & Sat 10:00-18:30, Thu 10:00-19:00

CONCRETE

018

35a Marshall Street, W1F 7EX
020 7434 4546
www.concretelondon.com
Tube: Oxford Circus
Open: Mon-Fri 11:00-19:00, Sat 11:00-18:30

Concrete photography by Naughty James

Concrete boutique is a venture by a fashion PR agency of the same name, so the men's and womenswear collections stocked here will have been seen on London Fashion Week catwalks as well as the pages of the top style magazines in the country. Stocking a stellar list of British and European labels, you'll find clothing and accessories by all the LFW greats including Jean Pierre Braganza, Ashish, Preen, Robert Carey Williams, Unconditional, Marjan Pejoski and Victim.

The Dispensary · 019

9 Newburgh Street, W1 7RB
020 7287 8145
www.thedispensary.net
Tube: Oxford Circus
Open: Mon-Sat 10:30-18:30, Thu 10:30-19:30, Sun 12:00-17:00

Independent fashion boutique, The Dispensary has been an essential retail destination in London for nearly 15 years. Its knack for hunting down the cooler, rarer labels has ensured a loyal clientele in both Notting Hill – where the first Dispensary launched in 1994 – and in its second home in Soho. Each store presents stock targeted at its local demographic, so in this womenswear-only branch, you'll find edgier collections from designers like Ivana Helsinki, Maria Bonita, Mine, Ciel and From Somewhere, along with the boutique's own label, Dispensary. The Notting Hill store stocks women's and menswear, accessories and footwear by high profile designers such as Servanne Gaxotte, Orla Kiely, and Without Prejudice.

THE DISPENSARY: Notting Hill is at 200 Kensington Park Road, W11 1VR
T: 020 7727 8797. Tube: Notting Hill Gate

Dover Street Market · 020

17-18 Dover Street, W1S 4LT
020 7518 0680
www.doverstreetmarket.com
Tube: Green Park
Open: Mon-Wed, Fri & Sat 11:00-18:00, Thu 11:00-19:00

Comme des Garçons founder and designer, Rei Kawakubo is the creator of this hipster-haven, dedicated to art, music, photography and fashion. The Dover Street Market (DSM) is housed in a Georgian building in Mayfair and encompasses six floors of industrially-designed retail and studio space. In addition to some of the most awesome store installations you're ever likely to see, expect to find stock from the latest and greatest designer talent out there. Its featured labels list reads like a who's who of creative brilliance: Gareth Pugh, Christopher Kane, Raf Simons, Boudicca, Kitsuné, not to mention the Comme des Garçons ranges, plus one-off collections by the likes of Chloë Sevigny — exclusive to DSM. LA vintage expert, Decades, resides here, and you'll also enjoy photography by major names including Nick Knight. If that's not enough to tempt you, DSM hosts live music performances and events in-store.

Dispensary photography by Naughty James

Dover Street Market photography courtesy of Dover Street Market

01 & 02 DPMHI photography by Keex

DPMHI   021

2-3 Great Pultney Street, W1F 9LY
020 7494 7550
www.dpmhi.com
Tube: Oxford Circus
Open: Mon-Sat 11:00-19:00, Thu 11:00-20:00

Blurring the lines between Harajuku, Tokyo and Soho, London, the DPMHI store is pure eye-candy featuring over four floors of product. A destination-cum-gallery for foot soldiers, Futura canvases burn the walls, oversized Unkle Kubricks pose menacingly, and Be@rbrick vending machines await your loose change. Patterned floors add to the insane attention to detail you come to expect from Maharishi, as do exclusive collaborations with Futura Labs, Nike and Michael Lau, and a well-sourced selection of art books. Creativity at its finest.

Foot Patrol

022

16a St Anne's Court, W1F 0BG
020 7734 1795
www.foot-patrol.com
Tube: Tottenham Court Road
Open: Mon-Fri 11:00-19:00, Sat 11:00-18:00

Hidden down a small back alley in the heart of Soho, Foot Patrol is sneaker HQ for London footwear fanatics. If it's a limited release you're after: Nike, Adidas, Vans, New Balance, whatever, these guys have it. You won't find the shoes here in any other stores, so if you're one of the sneaker obsessive types like us, this little emporium is as close to heaven on earth as you're going to get. The temptation to blow your entire credit card on these caged models is huge, so choose carefully and try to limit yourself to just one pair, if you can.

Fred Perry

023

Thomas Neal Centre, Earlham Street, WC2H 9LD
020 7836 4513
www.fredperry.co.uk
Tube: Covent Garden
Open: Mon-Sat 10:30-19:00, Sun 12:00-17:00

Joining the dots between decades of UK youth cultures, Fred Perry is as British as afternoon tea and as iconic as the Queen. An integral ingredient in numerous subcultural uniforms for over forty years, the label has been adopted by the Mods, Punks and Skinheads, and the new wave and Britpop scenes. Its clean understated cool is as relevant today as it was then. A hugely important British fashion label, so go buy some.

The Hideout photography by Keex

The Hideout

024

7 Upper James Street, W1F 9DH
020 7437 4929
www.hideoutstore.com
Tube: Oxford Circus
Open: Mon-Fri 11:00-19:00, Sat 11:00-18:30

The original and still the best, The Hideout has been supplying discerning Londoners with exclusive streetwear for over ten years now. The store is known for being the first to bring rare Japanese brands like Visvim, WTAPS and Neighbourhood to the UK, as well as stocking notoriously hard-to-find labels like Supreme and Perks and Mini. With an international reputation as a leading retailer on the scene, you only ever find the newest product ranges here. Stock turnaround is swift, due to its limited quantities, so if you like it, buy it, because it won't be here in an hour — yes, it's that quick. Staff are helpful and friendly (so rare in stores like this), and its central location, just off the end of Carnaby Street, makes it surprisingly accessible, even for inexperienced brand hunters.

IF Music photography by Keex

Hurwundeki   025

34 Marshall Street, W1F 7E
020 7734 1050
www.hurwundeki.com
Tube: Oxford Circus
Open: Mon-Sat 11:00-19:00, Sun 12:00-17:00

Hurwundeki has two boutiques in London, each stocking an excellent range of independent men's and women's designers, along with its own label, choice vintage, and accessories from the Victorian period onwards. This is the newer and larger of the two stores, the original residing in the East End.

HURWUNDEKI (EAST)

98 Commercial Street, E1 6LZ, T: 020 7392 9194. Tube: Liverpool Street

IF Music   026

3 Green's Court, W1F 0HD
020 7437 4799
www.ifmusic.co.uk
Tube: Piccadilly Circus
Open: Mon-Thu & Sat 11:30-19:30, Fri 11:30-late, Sun 11:30-16:00

Hidden down a Soho back alley, IF has a reputation as the biggest broken beat dealer in Europe, attracting a slew of domestic and international DJs like Gilles Peterson and Sir Norman Jay. Fronted by Jean-Claude Thompson from the Amalgamation of Soundz, IF continues to supply harder-to-find releases from nu soul and hip hop through to broken beat and disco. Art, books, CDs, DVDs and clothing are also on sale.

Kokon to Zai 027

57 Greek Street, W1D 3DX
020 7434 1316
www.kokontozai.co.uk
Tube: Tottenham Court Road
Open: Mon-Sat 11:00-19:30, Sun 12:00-18:00

Part fashion. Part music. Kokon to Zai manages to combine bleeding edge fashion designers with an equally style-conscious selection of music. One of the best boutiques in London for fashion, Kokon to Zai is where you can catch the most exciting designers under one roof. From KTZ and subversive designer, Noki, to Jeremy Scott, Cassette Playa, Henrik Vibscov and Marjan Pejoski, this place is the first port of call for London's influential. Musically, it specialises in everything electro, covering nu wave to no wave like no other, and along with its sister store in Paris, stocks a satisfying range of the latest imports and cheeky bootlegs. Although vinyl prices can be slightly higher than normal, Kokon to Zai is an essential visit and usually results in finding something that no one else is going to have in their record bag.

Liberty 028

214-220 Regent Street, W1B 5AH
020 7734 1234
www.liberty.co.uk
Tube: Oxford Circus
Open: Mon-Thu 10:00-21:00, Fri & Sat 10:00-20:00, Sun 12:00-18:00

Opening in 1874, Liberty of London is one of the world's oldest and most distinguished department stores. Its iconic Tudor façade is one of the capital's most famous retail landmarks, but within this historic building beats the heart of a cutting edge contemporary store, stocking a highly-edited range of men's and women's couture fashions, accessories, beauty products and designer homeware. No one can come to London without visiting this amazing store.

Sneakers

London is one of the world's top sneaker cities. The culture here now is as rich and diverse as any globally; hell, it's certainly the best in Europe (we don't care what you've heard, London's better). There was a time when footwear fetishists looked enviously to Japan, drooling at the exclusive releases that would only find their way to British shores as wildly overpriced imports. Nowadays, however, there's very little that a footwear aficionado looking for models and styles beyond the mainstream, can't get their grubby little hands on (or rather, feet into), due to London's array of high-minded retailers.

BEST SNEAKER STORES

Magma

8 Earlham Street, WC2H 9RY
020 7240 8498
www.magmabooks.com
Tube: Covent Garden
Open: Mon-Sat 10:00-19:00, Sun 12:00-18:00

Exclusively stocking creative arts and culture publications, Magma is our preferred independent bookshop in this city. Representing the very best in print media, the small and inviting shop constantly strives to provide its customers with cutting edge art, fashion and design literature. One of each book is available to flick through with box-fresh sealed copies to purchase, so no dog-eared publications in sight. With a price range to suit every pocket, you can pick up reading material for your tube journey for less than a Zone 1 single, or splash out on a beautiful book for £40. It's hard to walk out empty handed. Further along the road at no. 16 Earlham Street, you'll find Magma's product store, and there's a second Magma bookshop in Clerkenwell.

029

MAGMA (EAST):
117-119 Clerkenwell Road, EC1R 5BY. T: 020 7242 9503
01 & 02 Magma photography by Keex

Marshmallow Mountain

030

Ground Floor, Kingly Court, W1B 5PW
020 7434 9498
www.marshmallowmountain.com
Tube: Oxford Circus
Open: Mon-Wed 11:00-19:00, Thu-Sat
11:00-20:00, Sun 12:00-18:00

Marshmallow Mountain is a favourite vintage retail spot for Londoners. Full of dresses, furs, jewellery, sunglasses, hats and footwear, there are always amazing pieces on sale here. Needless to say, turnover of stock is fast which ensures a constant stream of new arrivals. It's a good job then that Marshmallow Mountain's founder, Kechi, is a vintage connoisseur who collects thousands of such items. It's reasonably priced too, considering the superb condition of the garments.

OPPOSITE: Marshmallow Mountain photography by Naughty James

Nike Town 032

236 Oxford Street, W1C 1DE
020 7612 0800
www.nike.com
Tube: Oxford Circus
Open: Mon-Wed 10:00-19:00, Thu-Sat 10:00-20:00, Sun 12:00-18:00

New Era 031

72-74 Brewer Street, W1F 9JG
020 7734 5950
www.neweracap.co.uk
Tube Piccadilly Circus
Open: Mon-Sat 12:00-19.00, Sun 12.00-18.00

The iconic headwear label's first European flagship store carries a large range of 59FIFTY product, much of it exclusive to the store. As well as its signature ranges, the store also sells the fashion lines created with New Era partners such as Mishka NYC and Stüssy.

Now, we know Nike Town needs no introductions: a huge temple of retail filled with every imaginable Nike product from across the sporting spectrum. But that is not to say that they are all created equal. We, after all, are in London, a global fashion capital, and therefore enjoy certain benefits that come with that, which in this case, means being one of a handful of locations to have an in-store NikeID design studio. We think that's worth a visit alone.

01 & 02 New Era photograph courtesy of New Era

03 Nike photograph courtesy of Nike

Playlounge 035

19 Beak Street, W1F 9RF
020 7287 7073
www.playlounge.co.uk
Tube: Oxford Circus
Open: Mon-Sat 11:00-19:00, Sun 12:00-17:00

At Playlounge, both children and adults are treated as equals so long as they share an appreciation for art and design-driven toys. Selling products from around the globe, the stock moves between incredible works of art, collectable action figures, and toys which have been manufactured as innovative educational tools. Whatever your level of interest in toys, you will find the largest selection in London at Playlounge. The store also has a close association with comic and graphic art, and was behind the Zarjaz! 2000AD art exhibition which brought together forty artists and designers including James Jarvis and Pete Fowler.

Number 22 033

22 Carnaby Street, W1F 7DB
020 7734 1690
www.swear-london.com
Tube: Oxford Circus
Open: Mon-Sat 11:00-19:00, Sun 13:00-18:00

Designer London footwear label, S**R's flagship store on Carnaby Street is the perfect place to address your shoe needs. Not for the faint-of-fashion-heart, S**R's styles and colours make a seriously bold style statement, ensuring they're a regular fixture on the feet of celebrities and hipsters alike. You'll find the entire range here, including their innovative collaborative lines, designed in conjunction with other leading fashion labels.

Phonica Records 034

51 Poland Street, W1F 7LZ
020 7025 6070
www.phonicarecords.co.uk
Tube: Oxford Circus
Open: Mon-Wed 11:30-19:30, Thu-Fri 11:30-20:00
Sat 11:30-19:30, Sun 12:00-18:00

An independent stalwart of the new generation record stores, Phonica addresses the love of music and art with an in-house gallery, a huge art space (just off Carnaby Street), plenty of listening decks and a lazy leather couch area, complete with reading material courtesy of London's underground press. Across the board genres are catered for from disco to folk, nu jazz to techno, with a particularly impressive stock of cutting edge house, electro and electronica. Knowledgeable and enthusiastic staff are always on hand, as is a selection of limited tees, CDs, books and DVDs, to spur creativity.

Playlounge photography by Keex

number 22

Number 22
22 Carnaby Street
London W1F 7DB
0207 7341690
www.swear-london.com

pm People's market

S***R

PPQ

036

47 Conduit Street, W1S 2YP
020 7494 9789
www.ppqclothing.com
Tube Oxford Circus
Open: Mon-Wed 10:30-18:30, Thu 10:30-19:00, Fri & Sat 10:30-18:30

It started as a collective of artists, musicians and designers working together back in 1992. Over fifteen years later, Amy Molyneaux's and Percy Parker's fashion label, PPQ enters its fourth year at London Fashion Week; the record label 1-2-3-4 Records (with Sonic Mook's Sean McLusky) is going strong, and the team can lay claim to art collaborations with the likes of Sam Taylor-Wood. A directional British fashion label, PPQ has been a huge hit with London's style pack since it launched. Find out why by visiting this flagship, where you'll find the entire PPQ collection.

Puma

037

52-55 Carnaby Street, W1F 9QE
020 7439 0221
www.puma.com
Tube: Oxford Circus
Open: Mon-Sat 10:00-19:00

We've been in love with Puma sportswear ever since we watched 1984 movie, *Beat Street*. Of course we wanted the Rock Steady Crew to win that b-boy battle at The Roxy but you can't argue that the New York City Breakers looked dope in Puma. That styling with its heavy colour clashes was a golden era for the brand, and at Puma's store on Carnaby Street, many of these early designs can be found alongside the latest releases and exclusive collaborations.

Selfridges 038

400 Oxford Street, W1A 1AB
0800 123 400
www.selfridges.com
Tube: Bond Street. Open: Mon-Wed 09:30-20:00, Thu 09:30-21:00
Fri & Sat 09:30-20:00, Sun 12.00-18.00

Catering to 90% of your shopping needs, department store, Selfridges boasts six massive floors of fashion and food, homeware, beauty, footwear and leisure. There are thousands of high-end, streetwear, and lesser-known independent labels here, along with several good vintage concessions. The shoe section takes up over half of one of the floors, stocking plenty of well-known brands like Gina and Jimmy Choo. Its overwhelmingly-scented health & beauty section retails all the top make-up, skincare and perfume brands. The basement area houses books and a record store, while the homeware department is a mix of contemporary and traditional designs with a vast range of household items on offer including soft furnishings and lighting. In addition to all this, there is a food hall, a beauty salon and nearly twenty restaurants, cafes, bars and snack stops dotted throughout the building — which should give you an indication of the scale of this place.

Size? 039

33-34 Carnaby Street, W1F 7DW
020 7287 4016
www.size-online.co.uk
Tube: Oxford Circus
Open: Mon-Wed & Fri 10:00-19:30, Thu 10:00-20:00, Sun 12:00-18:00

The phrase inscribed on the gates of hell in Dante's 'Divine Comedy': "*Abandon all hope, ye who enter here*," should also adorn the doors of Size?. A one-stop-shop for the latest sneakers, it lures you in with all the pretty colours, and then traps you with its choice of, literally, hundreds of shoes. Resistance is futile. The dizzying selection tends to be on the mainstream side, but frequent store exclusives and limited editions make it popular with serious sneaker-heads, as well as those just looking for new shoes. You can't go shopping in London without checking one of their stores out, but be prepared... the *colours*!

SIZE? also has stores in: Covent Garden: 37a Neal Street, WC2H 9PR, T: 020 7379 9768
Notting Hill: 200 Portobello Road, W11 1LB, T: 020 7792 8494

Slam City Skates 040

16 Neal's Yard, WC2H 9DP
020 7240 0928
www.slamcity.com
Tube: Covent Garden
Open: Mon-Sat 11:00-19:00, Sun 12:00-17:00

The most famous skate shop in the capital, Slam City Skates is as synonymous with the London skate scene as South Bank, Stockwell, and rain. Run by skateboarders for skateboarders (Unabombers' Chris Pulman manages the store), it's not unusual to find the odd Pro' or Am' helping out behind the counter. A densely-packed treasure trove of skate booty, you'll find the more unique companies and labels that Europe and the US has to offer. A good range of UK decks adorn the back wall with trucks, wheels and DVDs under the counter.

Sounds of the Universe 041

7 Broadwick Street, W1F 0DA
020 7734 3430
www.soundsoftheuniverse.com
Tube: Oxford Circus
Open: Mon-Sat 11:00-19:30

When we're on Desert Island Discs, our luxury item will be Sounds of the Universe. Better known as Soul Jazz, after the mighty record label which finds its home here, this store sees reggae 45s sit comfortably with deep electronica, as disco 12"s while away the hours with their house grandchildren. In the basement, you'll find second-hand jazz, Brazilian and Latin swapping dance steps with rare soul and dirty funk 45s. Here, the guiding principle is quantities of quality.

Souvenir 042

53 Brewer Street, W1F 9UY
020 7287 9877
www.souvenirboutique.co.uk
Tube: Oxford Circus
Open: Mon-Wed, Fri & Sat 11:00-19:00, Thu 11:00-19:30, Sun 12:00-18:00

Souvenir's founders, Anna and Anthony, fill this tiny boutique with rare and exclusive catwalk pieces, making it a top choice for the style-conscious and monied. Featuring the most outstanding garments to come off the runway, you'll find lines by Vivienne Westwood, PPQ, Ashish, Chloé, A.P.C and Viktor & Rolf plus accessories, jewellery and footwear.

STELLA MCCARTNEY 043

30 Bruton Street, W1J 6QR
020 7518 3100
www.stellamccartney.com
Tube: Green Park
Open: Mon-Wed 10:00-18:00, Thu 10:00-19:00, Fri & Sat 10:00-18:00

Situated in 11,000 sq ft of four-storey, Grade II-listed Georgian townhouse splendour, no one can accuse Miss McCartney of not taking her fashion seriously. Her London flagship carries her entire product range, and even if you can't afford to shop here, go anyway and have a look at the store, it's beautiful.

STÜSSY 044

19 Earlham Street, WC2 9LL
020 7836 9418
www.stussystore.co.uk
Tube: Covent Garden
Open: Mon-Sat 11:00-19:00, Sun 13:00-17:30

The elder statesman of global streetwear, Shaun Stussy's flagship UK store carries a complete range of the brand's threads, accessories, footwear and limited store exclusives. It's an absolute necessity for streetwear and sneaker-heads, period.

TOPSHOP 045

Oxford Circus, 36-38 Great Castle Street, W1W 81G
020 7499 2917
www.topshop.com
Tube: Oxford Circus
Open: Mon-Sat 09:00-20:00, Sun 12:00-18:00

Topshop featuring the Kate Moross collaboration: photography by Keex

The world's largest fashion store, Topshop is a UK high street institution. With a production turnaround of just six weeks, Topshop is the most up-to-date fashion outlet in London, with catwalk-influenced designs, sold at affordable prices. Designers are jumping on board too, with everyone from indie illustrator, Kate Moross to supermodel, Kate Moss collaborating with the store on clothing collections. The Boutique is dedicated to lines by major 'designers-for-Topshop' like Christopher Kane and Preen while the basement offers concessions by smaller labels plus a good vintage section. In addition to a cafe, nail bar, and a large footwear department, you'll find just about anything in this flagship from wigs and duvet covers to lingerie, jewellery and sweets.

TWOSEE 046

21 Foubert's Place, W1F 7QE
020 7494 3813
www.twoseelife.com
Tube: Covent Garden
Open: Mon-Sat 10:00-18:00, Sun 12:00-18:00

A stunning boutique which offers conceptual fashion labels for men and women. Skilled in both identifying the next big designers and unearthing must-have clothing and accessories from around the world, Antonio Ciutto (architect turned designer) and Aimee McWilliams (an award-winning Central St Martins graduate), are typical of the forward-thinking designers who make their UK retail debut at this boutique. A strong appreciation of art and photography guarantees some great in-store exhibitions and installations, and there's always someone super-knowledgeable working here, whether it's a stylist, or Anthony Stephinson — the boutique's charming buyer/manager/creative director. Anthony ensures that TwoSee is the first European stockist of designers-of-the-moment like Patrik Rzepski — the New York native responsible for dressing Chloë Sevigny. He also buys-in cutting edge garments and accessories by Jeremy Scott, Preen, Jean Pierre Braganza and Burfitt.

UNIQLO 047

311 Oxford Street, W1C 2HP
020 7290 7701
www.uniqlo.co.uk
Tube: Oxford Circus or Bond Street
Open: Mon-Wed 10:00-20:00, Thu 10.00-21:00, Fri & Sat 10:00-21:00, Sun 12.00-18:00

The Japanese label, famous for its affordable and stylish clothing, has recently stepped up its presence in London, opening a flagship store on Oxford Street. Bringing effortless, understated style and attention to detail to the capital's high street, Japanese design firm Wonderwall — who created the various Bathing Ape stores around the world — was given the task of creating the shop's interior. Great for wardrobe staples.

UPPER PLAYGROUND 048

31 Kingly Street, W1B 5BQ
020 7734 8705
www.upperplayground.com
Tube: Oxford Circus
Open: Mon-Sat 10:00-19:00, Sun 11:00-18:00

One of only two Upper Playground stores outside the US, this is the UK's flagship, and the only dedicated European location to stock the art and apparel brand's entire range of products. A must-visit for art aficionados, Upper Playground, (and its Fifty24SF gallery over in the US) has been an instrumental force in pushing the contemporary art and streetwear scene for over 10 years. This outstanding addition to London's retail landscape offers artist film, clothing, bags, furniture and books from the likes of Jeremy Fish, Sam Flores, David Choe, Anthony Lister, Chuey, The London Police, Craola and Albert Reyes.

TwoSee photography by Keex

VICTIM 049

33 Marshall Street, W1F 7EX
020 7494 4044
www.victimfashionst.com
Tube: Oxford Circus
Open: Mon-Sat 12:00-18:30

Acclaimed womenswear designer, Mei Hui Liu introduces a taste of art school creativity to West End consumers with her new Soho boutique. The Fashion Week runway regular showcases her outstanding vintage-inspired collections at this store, along with accessories and shoes by Alpha Omega. Taiwan-born Mei Hui launched her first store on east London's Fashion Street back in 2001, which became one of the coolest in the area. Invitations followed to collaborate with Topshop for their designer series, and she has ongoing catwalk shows at LFW.

VINYL JUNKIES 051

92 Berwick Street, W1F 0QF
020 7439 2923
www.vinyl-junkies.com
Tube: Piccadilly Circus
Open: Mon-Sat 11:00-19:00, Sun 12:00-18:00

If you spend more time listening to vinyl than you do showering, then Vinyl Junkies will reduce you to a strip wash. The record store stocks a massive amount of quality vinyl spanning house, tech, funk and disco plus a great selection of rarities and reissues. The service is second-to-none with plenty of listening posts and a hassle-free atmosphere. Perhaps that's why the likes of Todd Terry, Carl Craig, Derrick May and countless other music professionals shop here... or maybe they just hang around to see what we're buying.

Vivienne Westwood 050

44 Conduit Street, W1S 2YL
020 7439 1109
www.viviennewestwood.com
Tube: Oxford Circus or Bond Street
Open: Mon-Wed, Fri & Sat 10:00-18:00, Thu 10:00-19:00

Dame of British fashion, Vivienne Westwood has three stores in the capital, each stocking her Brit-centric creations. The store on Davies Street brings us the designer's Gold Label couture while the flagship Conduit Street outlet offers both Red and Gold Label along with her menswear collection. You'll find all the trademark pieces from the celebrated platform shoes to her beautifully-designed corsets. For high-end British fashion, nobody does it better. If you want to see Westwood's original work, head down to her first (and best) shop, World's End on the King's Road.

BRANCHES: 430 King's Road, SW10 0LG. T: 020 7352 6551
6 Davies Street, W1K 3DN. T: 020 7629 3757

Wyld Pytch 052

51 Lexington Street, W1F 9HL
020 7434 3472
www.wyldpytch.com
Tube: Piccadilly Circus
Open: Mon-Sat 11:00-19:00

Record store, Wyld Pytch is a cornerstone of the London hip hop scene, serving the community for over 15 years now. This Soho institution stocks current UK & US hip hop and RnB releases, along with mix CDs, DVDs, and own-brand clothing. Particular strengths lie with club tracks and regular deliveries of US promos and white label imports. Not content with just providing hip hop fans with wax, Digger, the main man behind Wyld Pytch, develops urban artists for Warner and Sony, dabbles in music publishing and set up African funk label, 51 Lex Records. Back the bid for this playa's MBE for hip hop services rendered.

store
GALLERY

magazine ■ london listings ■ news & reviews

pimpguides.com

MICHIKO
KOSHINO
SHARON
WAUCHOB
RICK OWENS
MARTIN
MARGIELA
GUSTAVO LINS
GUIDI
SCHA
ORKSHDW
YEN JEANS
0044
JULIUS
GUIDA MIDANI
VLEC
ISAAC SELLAM
PLEASURE
PRINCIPLE
CHRISTIAN
LUPPI
MARSELL
INTOXICA
GIORGIO
BRATO
NICOLAS AND
MARK
SUE STEMP
TILLMANN
LAUTERBACH
MALLONI
SERGIO PERRERO
HTC
REINHARD PLANK
INTOXICA DENIM
KAMINMA
CHINAMI
UNRULY
TO TANKER
ILARIA NISTRI

55DSL

10a Newburgh Street, W1F 7RN. T: 020 7439 1300
W: www.55DSL.com Tube: Oxford Circus
Open: Mon-Wed, Fri & Sat 10:30-19:00
Thu 10:30-19:30, Sun 12:00-18:00

Diesel's younger streetwear spin-off, 55DSL has its own dedicated store carrying the full range of 55DSL apparel and accessories including the label's newly-launched sunglasses collection. The recently-redesigned space also has in-store exhibitions and collaborations with artists including Adam Neate and The London Police.

59 Broadwick Street

59 Broadwick Street, W1F 9QQ. T: 020 7434 3686
W: www.59broadwickstreet.com
Tube: Oxford Circus. Open: Mon-Sat 10:00-19:00

59 Broadwick Street is the concept boutique of internationally-renowned fashion designer, Michiko Koshino. At this gallery store, you will find some of the most interesting labels to come out of Japan and Europe including 0044, Julius, and Rick Owens, along with Koshino's own high-end collections and diffusion lines.

Addict

3 Earlham Street, WC2H 9LL. T: 020 7379 9348
W: www.addict.co.uk Tube: Tottenham Court Road
Open: Mon-Sat 11:00-19:00, Sun 12:00-18:00

The British streetwear brand's official flagship store is an impressive 1200 sq ft, architect-designed space, located in the heart of Covent Garden. Stocking, as one would expect, the entire mens- and womenswear collection, accessories, luggage and their exclusive artist collaborative lines, there are also some great store exclusives such as beanbags, tents and artworks.

PHOTOGRAPHY

01 & 02 59 Broadwick Street photography
courtesy of 59 Broadwick Street
03 & 04 Addict photography courtesy
of Addict
05 American Apparel photography courtesy of
American Apparel, Inc
06 BM Records photography by Keex

AMERICAN APPAREL has stores in Shoreditch,
Soho, Kensington and Portobello. For the full review, see page 33

BEYOND RETRO'S East End store is at 110-112
Cheshire Street, E2 6EJ. T: 020 7613 3636

Agent Provocateur

6 Broadwick Street, W1F 8HL. T: 020 7439 0229
W: www.agentprovocateur.com Tube: Oxford Circus
Open: Mon-Sat 11:00-19:00, Thu 11:00-20:00
Sun 12:00-17:00

The 007 of luxurious lingerie, Joe
Corre is a chip off the old block (his
mother is Vivienne Westwood),
designing erotic underwear along with
co-founder, Serena Rees. Agent Provo-
cateur also stocks sex toys, accessories
and the infamous pom-pom mules.

American Apparel

142-144 Oxford Street, W1D 1NB. T: 020 7631 1792
W: www.americanapparel.net Tube: Oxford Circus
Open: Mon-Sat 10:00-20:00, Sat 12:00-18:00, Sun
11:00-12:00

The world's leading retailer of ethi-
cally-produced fashion, American
Apparel's brightly-coloured and endlessly wearable hoodies, tees, sweats
and accessories have become the
casual staples of every style-conscious wardrobe in London.

Ben Sherman

50 Carnaby Street, W1F 9QA. T: 020 7437 2031
W: www.bensherman.com Tube: Oxford Circus
Open: Mon-Wed, Fri & Sat 10:00-19:00
Thu 10:00-20:00, Sun 12:00-18:00

This British label has been kitting out
youth subcultures for five decades,
worn by Mods, Skinheads and countless influential bands including The Jam
and The Specials. For a taste of London
youth culture, past and present, head
down to this flagship store, located,
quite rightly, on Carnaby Street.

Beyond Retro

58-59 Great Marlborough Street, W1F 7JY
T: 020 7434 1406. W: www.beyondretro.com
Tube: Oxord Circus. Open: Daily 10:00-18:00

Beyond Retro introduces a slimmed-
down version of its mighty East End
vintage emporium with a second store
in Soho. As with their first and larger
outlet off Brick Lane, expect an excellent selection of low-priced vintage
clothing, footwear and accessories
from the 1940s onwards.

BM Records

25 D'Arblay Street, W1F 8EJ. T: 020 7437 0478
W: www.bm-soho.com Tube: Oxford Circus
Open: Mon-Wed & Sat 11:00-19:00
Thu & Fri 11:00-20:00

House music's longest standing groove
emporium has been retailing underground dance releases to Londoners for
nearly two decades. Co-owned by Azuli
Records head honcho, David Piccioni,
and UK drum 'n' bass DJ, Nicky Black-
market, this store has a wide selection
of 12"s covering electro, soulful house,
drum 'n' bass, grime and bassline.

Boxfresh

13 Shorts Gardens, WC2H 9AT. T: 020 7240 4742
W: www.boxfresh.co.uk Tube: Covent Garden
Open: Mon-Wed, Fri & Sat 10:00-18:30
Thu 10:00-19:00, Sun 12:00-18:00

One of the first British streetwear brands
to gain global recognition, Boxfresh has
been around since 1989. A pioneer of UK
urban style, its flagship store in Covent
Garden — a slick two-floor space — is the
culmination of nearly 20 years in the
game. It's hard to believe it started life as
a market stall selling screen-printed vintage tees back in the day.

CARHARTT stores: Covent Garden: 56 Neal Street, WC2H 9PA, T: 020 7836 5659 Tube: Covent Garden. **Carhartt Warehouse:** 18 Ellingfort Road (off Mare Street), E8 3PA T: 020 8986 8875. Tube/Rail: Hackney Central rail or Bethnal Green tube

Carhartt

15-17 Earlham Street, WC2H 9LL. T: 020 7836 1551 W: www.thecarharttstore.co.uk Tube: Covent Garden. Open: Mon-Sat 11:00-19:00, Sun 12:00-1800

The flagship store of one of the world-leading workwear-turned-streetwear brands. You know the deal: quality materials, minimal designs in camo and earthy tones now running alongside brighter colourways. Live music performances and art exhibitions regularly feature in-store with top UK artists like Will Barras & Steff Plaetz.

Chateau Roux

17 Newburgh Street, W1F 7RZ. T: 0871 200 3351 W: www.chateauroux.co.uk Tube: Oxford Circus Open: Mon-Wed & Fri 11:00-19:00, Thu 12:00-20:00, Sat 11:00-19:00, Sun 11:00-18:00

This exciting new clothing and jewellery label launched its first store in Soho late 2007. The incredible design-led jewellery and bespoke handprinted slogan tees, hoodies and sweats, are worn by artists such as M.I.A and New Young Pony Club as well as the capital's indie kids.

Cinch

5 Newburgh Street, W1F 7RG. T: 020 7287 4941 Tube: Oxford Circus. Open: Mon-Sat 11:00-18:30 Sun 13:00-16:00

Essentially a Levi's concept boutique, this shop/gallery stocks the brand's Red Tab and vintage lines, specialising in limited edition denim products, collaborative lines with streetwear brands like Stüssy, and occasional collections from other designers.

Converse

33-34 Carnaby Street (upstairs at Size?), W1F 7DW. T: 020 7287 4016. W: www.converse.com Tube: Oxford Circus. Open: Mon-Wed & Fri 10:00-19:30, Thu 10:00-20:00, Sun 12:00-18:00

If Converse All Stars are your thing, get yourself down to Carnaby Street to their flagship London store, housed upstairs at sneaker outlet, Size? This concession is littered with hard-to-find colourways and limited editions you won't find anywhere else.

Dr. Martens

17-19 Neal Street, WC2H 9PU. T: 020 7240 7555 Tube: Covent Garden. Open: Mon-Wed 10:00-19:00, Thu-Sat 10:00-20:00, Sun 11:00-18:00

Synonymous globally with youth, numerous subcultural movements and their associated styles have had Dr. Martens at the centre of their aesthetic. Dr. Martens and its iconic DM boot (a 20th century design classic) have symbolised the rebellion of youth for over forty years.

The Face

1 Marlborough Court, W1F 7EE. T: 020 7439 4706 Tube: Oxford Circus. Open: Mon-Sat 10:00-18.30 Sun 12:00-17:00

A shrine to Mod culture and 1960s fashion, you'll find all the classic brands and sharp styles here. The Face stocks signature Mod and Ska clothing, footwear and accessories including bowling shoes, Harringtons, Crombies and monkey boots.

Fenchurch

36 Earlham Street, WC2H 9LL. T: 020 7240 1880 W: www.fenchurch.com Tube: Covent Garden Open: Mon-Sat 10:00-19:00, Sun 12:00-18:00

The internationally-renowned skater-run streetwear label, Fenchurch has its flagship store in Covent Garden, carrying the entire range of apparel and accessories for men and women.

Firetrap

21-23 Earlham Street, WC2H 9LL. T: 020 7395 1830. W: www.firetrap.com Tube: Covent Garden Open: Mon-Wed, Fri & Sat 10:00-19:00, Thu 10:00-19:30, Sun 12:00-18:00

Firetrap is a leading jeanswear label in the UK, and this flagship store even has a dedicated-fit denim specialist to ensure you find the perfect pair of jeans. The Firetrap range crosses five divisions: Men and Womenswear Collections, Firetrap Black Seal (denim collection), Accessories and Footwear, all of which you'll find here.

Harriet's Muse

Unit 1.12, Kingly Court, W1B 5PW. T: 020 7734 1773. W: www.harrietsmuse.com Tube: Oxford Circus. Open: Mon-Sat 11:00-19:00, Sun 12:00-17:00

We don't know who Harriet's muse is, but she must be pretty inspirational if the designs in this boutique are anything to go by. Stunning made-to-measure corsets with matching skirts (think Vivienne Westwood) sit alongside an opulent abundance of lines made from the highest quality fabrics. Better still, only ten of each design is produced, to ensure exclusivity.

PHOTOGRAPHY
01 Fenchurch photograph courtesy of Fenchurch
02 Harriet's Muse photography by Nosca
03 Lazy Oaf photograph courtesy of Lazy Oaf
04 Microzine photography by Keex

H&M

261-271 Regent Street (Oxford Circus), W1R 7PA T: 020 7493 4004. Tube: Oxford Circus. Open: Mon-Wed, Fri & Sat 09:00-20:00, Thu 09:00-21:00 Sun 12:00-18:00

No other store rivals Swedish retailer, H&M in introducing the latest fashions at the lowest prices. Ever since Stella McCartney, Viktor & Rolf, Karl Lagerfeld and Roberto Cavalli jumped on board for collaborations, H&M has become one of the most sought-after destinations for casual wardrobe basics and fashion-wear in Europe.

HMV

150 Oxford Street, W1D 1DJ. T: 0845 602 7800 W: www.hmvgroup.com Tube: Tottenham Court Road Open: Mon-Wed, Fri & Sat 09:00-20:30 Thu 09:00-21:00, Sun 12:00-18:00

Music behemoth, HMV boasts the biggest selection of music in the capital. Its Oxford Street flagship is the largest record store in the world, and also one of the oldest shops on this strip, arriving here in 1921.

Joie

37 Marshall Street, W1F 7EZ T: 020 7434 3423 Tube: Oxford Circus. Open: Mon-Sat 11:00-19:00 Sun 12:00-16:30

Womenswear boutique, Joie is a word of mouth, 'in the know' kind of place. Everything about this store is perfect, from the imaginative window displays (including 1970s reconditioned mannequins) to the beautifully-designed dresses, skirts, tops and jackets. Founder, Joie Readman's passion and talent has made this boutique one of the prettiest in the capital.

Koh Samui

65-67 Monmouth Street, WC2H 9DG. T: 020 7240 4280. Tube: Covent Garden. Open: Mon-Sat 10:00-18:30, Sun 12:00–17:00

This renowned boutique sells high-end clothing, shoes and accessories from leading designers like Stella McCartney, Chloé, Matthew Williamson, Missoni and Balenciaga, for women, and Buddhist Punk, Marc Jacobs and Veronique Branquinho, for men. It's also a good place to pick up label newcomers before they hit the mainstream.

Original Levi's Store

174 Regent Street, W1R 5DF. T: 020 7292 2500 W: www.levi.co.uk Tube: Oxford Circus. Open: Mon-Wed, Fri & Sat 10:00-19:00, Thu 10:00- 20:00, Sun 12:00-18:00

This is the flagship store of the international denim brand, where you'll find a complete range of all the latest Levi collections.

Lazy Oaf

G4, Kingly Court, W1B 5PW. T: 020 7287 2060 W: www.lazyoaf.co.uk Tube: Oxford Circus Open: Mon-Sat 11:00-19:00, Sun 12:00-18:00

What launched as a series of sketches and tees by Gemma Shiel in 2001, has evolved into one of the capital's quirkiest little stores. Affordable fashion and accessories from new designers sit alongside the Lazy Oaf boutique's own-brand tees and sweats. You'll also find cute toys, badges, stationery, art, and a great range of rocker jewellery by Lady Luck Rules OK.

Maharishi

19 Floral Street, WC2E 9DS. T: 020 7836 3860 W: www.emaharishi.com Tube: Covent Garden Open: Mon-Sat 12:00-19:00, Sun 12:00-17:00

Maharishi is probably the UK's premier streetwear brand. The famous disruptive pattern material (camouflage, to you and me) clothing and designs have a huge following worldwide. Check out their HQ for some high-end goodies.

Microzine

Unit 1.2 Kingly Court, W1F 9PY. T: 020 7434 0909 Tube: Oxford Street Open: Mon-Sat 11:00-19:00 Sun 12:00-18:00

One-stop design store, Microzine meets the demands of the modern male, selling almost everything he might need and even things he didn't know he needed. Much of the product is exclusive to the store with limited edition clothing, footwear, technology goods and furniture on sale. Gas masks, gym equipment, toys, books, Raybans, scooters... it's all here.

Onitsuka Tiger

15 Newburgh Street, W1F 7RX. T: 020 7734 5157 W: www.onitsukatiger.co.uk Tube: Oxford Circus Open: Mon-Wed, Fri & Sat 11:00-19:00, Thu 11:00-19:30, Sun 12:00-17:00

This cult Japanese sports brand was made famous in the West by Bruce Lee who wore a yellow pair of their track shoes in his 1968 film, *Game of Death*. The small flagship store on Newburgh Street is compact, yet filled with exclusive styles you won't find anywhere else.

Pop Boutique

6 Monmouth Street, WC2H 9HB. T: 020 7497 5262. W: www.pop-boutique.com Tube: Covent Garden. Open: Mon-Sat 11:00-19:00 Sun 13:00-18:00

A retro boutique specialising in clothing, accessories and homewares from the 1950s to the '70s. This psychedelic store sells vintage pieces alongside their own Pop label tees and bags.

Sam Greenberg

Unit 1.7, Kingly Court, W1B 5PW. T: 020 7287 8474 W: www.samgreenbergvintage.co.uk Tube: Oxford Circus. Open: Mon-Wed & Fri 11:00-19:00, Thu 11:00-20:00, Sat 10:00-19:00, Sun 12:00-18:00

Sam Greenberg has been supplying vintage clothing, accessories and footwear to men and women in London since 1935. What started as a market stall on Petticoat Lane, is now a vintage fashion emporium with two outlets in the capital selling products which match the latest trends.

On the Beat Records

22 Hanway Street, W1T 1UH. T: 020 7637 8934 Tube: Tottenham Court Road. Open: Mon-Sat 11:00-19:00

If it wasn't for the vinyl labelled 1980s soul, we would have believed we were in 1976 on our first visit here. There are no listening posts, just dusty vinyl spanning punk, electro, soul, jazz, rock and so much more. If you're a DJ/collector, you probably already know this shop. If you're a producer, this place is great for rare samples.

R.D Franks

5 Winsley Street, W1W 8HG. T: 020 7636 1244 W: www.rdfranks.co.uk Tube: Oxford Circus Open: Mon-Fri 09:00-18:00

For the largest selection of fashion magazines and books in London, look no further than R.D Franks. The shop, which launched in 1877, is the only fashion bookshop in the country, stocking all the top international style glossies, trade directories, niche titles and rarities covering trend forecasting, design, trade, textiles, photography, graphics and illustration.

Sam Walker

65 Endell Street, WC2H 9AJ. T: 020 7240 9975 Tube: Covent Garden. Open: Mon-Sat 11:00-19:30 Sun 12:00-18:00

Sam Walker is an institution in these parts. Consistent in its offering of 1960s fashion, you'll find a good range of Mod-related apparel here. The store is set over two floors, but appears tiny due to the high and wide stacks of product which are crammed into every available space.

Paul Smith

40/44 Floral Street, WC2E 9DG. T: 020 7379 7133 W: www.paulsmith.co.uk Tube: Covent Garden Open: Mon-Wed 10:30-18:00, Thu 10:30-19:00, Fri 10:30-18:30, Sat 10:00-18:30, Sun 12:30-17:00

The flagship store of Britain's most iconic menswear designer, Paul Smith stocks the entire product range and previews his latest fashion collections, along with art, books, jewellery and accessories. Paul Smith also collaborates with graphic artists for exclusive runs, all of which you'll find here.

SAM GREENBERG has a second factory outlet in the East End at 64 Sclater Street, E1 6HR T: 020 7033 4045. Tube: Liverpool Street

BEST RECORD STORES

Phonica Records *page 86*
Pure Groove *page 124*
Rough Trade East *page 41*
Sound 323 *page 124*
Sounds of the Universe *page 89*

Shop@Maison Bertaux

27 Greek Street (basement), W1D 5DF. T: 0560 1151 584. W: www.shopatmaisonb.com Tube: Tottenham Court Road. Open: Tue-Sat 11:00-18:30

Housed in the basement of a Soho patisserie, this is a secret shopping destination for stylish locals. Collections by A.P.C, Eley Kishimoto and Sonia by Sonia Rykiel have been hand-picked by owners Max and Pippa. Vivienne Westwood pieces sit alongside Marc Jacobs, Hussein and Silas, and new designers and streetwear labels often join the rails.

Tabio

66 Neal Street, WC2H 9PA. T: 020 7836 3713
W: www.tabio.com Tube: Covent Garden
Open: Mon-Sat 10:00-19:30, Sun 12:00-18:00

Japanese retailer, Tabio exclusively stocks fashion socks in every style and colour combination imaginable. Prices are low and the variety is huge.

Twinkled

1.5 Kingly Court, W1B 5PW. T: 020 7734 1978
W: www.twinkled.net Tube: Oxford Circus
Open: Mon-Wed, Fri & Sat 11:00-19:00, Thu 11:00-20:00 Sun 12:00-18:00

Born over a decade ago from the marriage of its creators' self-confessed obsession with shopping, and a house bursting with the fruits of said obsession, vintage shop, Twinkled evolved from a one-stall car boot sale to a camped-up recreation room. In addition to selling one-off pieces from the 1950s to the 1980s, founders, Luke and Kevin are also a dab hand at interior design and can give your pad a retro makeover as part of their party hire service, personal fulfilling any 'look' or costume requirement that takes your fancy. If you're looking to have some fashion fun, delve into this giant prop box.

Twinkled is planning a rebrand, so the name of the store may have changed by the time you visit.

Sister Ray

34-35 Berwick Street, W1V 8RP. T: 020 7734 3297
W: www.sisterray.co.uk Tube: Oxford Circus
Open: Mon-Sat 09:30-20:00, Sun 12:00-18:00

One of London's most loved independent record stores, Sister Ray boasts a large back-catalogue of new and second-hand disco, soul, funk and jazz records (many of which are rare or out of print). This is a one-stop shop for all your crate-digging requirements with stock covering techno, house, punk, electro, hip hop, dubstep and new wave.

Urban Outfitters

200 Oxford Street, W1D 1NU. T: 020 7907 0815
W: www.urbanoutfitters.co.uk Tube: Oxford Circus
Open: Mon-Wed, Fri & Sat 10:00-20:00, Thu 10:00-21:00, Sun 12:00-18:00

This one-stop shopping emporium offers three floors of fashion labels, vintage, shoes, homeware, records, books and accessories for men and women. Their sales are excellent with product often marked down by 70%. There are additional branches in High Street Kensington and Covent Garden.

Vans

47 Carnaby Street, W1F 9PT. T: 020 7287 9235
W: www.vans.eu Tube: Oxford Circus. Open: Mon-Wed, Fri & Sat 10:00-19:00, Thu 10:00-20:00, Sun 12:00-18:00

Cemented in skateboard history, Vans' amazing team, and the rising popularity of old school skate shoes, has ensured that this brand is still going strong. Its flagship European store in Carnaby, offers two-floors of all things Vans, including exclusive colourways on those classic slip-ons.

Vintage Magazine Co.

39-43 Brewer Street, W1F 9UD. T: 020 7439 8525
W: www.vinmag.com Tube: Oxford Circus
Open: Mon-Thu 10:00-19:00, Fri & Sat 10:00-22:00, Sun 12:00-20:00

Two floors of vintage posters, magazines, photos, band tees and movie memorabilia from the 1950s onwards. Downstairs is dedicated to rare issues of style, music and porn magazines, and you're bound to see comics and glossies that didn't stand the test of time but which still hold a certain nostalgia. Collectors will love this place.

Wow Retro

10-14 Mercer Street, WC2H 9QA. T: 020 7379 5334
W: www.wowretro.co.uk Tube: Covent Garden
Open: Mon-Fri 11:30-18:30, Sat 11:00-19:00, Sun 12:30-17:30

You have to search this vintage boutique out, but once you've found it, you'll become a regular rummager. It mainly stocks 1960s and '70s retro gear and offers a great choice of footwear. Accessories for both sexes are the finest treasure in this chest, and the joy of the hunt is unbeatable.

CENTRAL ART

Art in central London is reflective of the wide cross-section of people that this part of town attracts. There's something for everyone: small art galleries sit alongside independent urban art dealers, and behemoths like The Tate Britain and The National Gallery. Then you've got the underground art courtesy of London's creative youth, which appears throughout the year in the form of temporary retail and exhibition spaces. And that's just the galleries. Streetwear boutiques often present in-store exhibitions, and annual events like Santa's Ghetto, which takes place in central London every December, sells limited edition work by leading graffiti artists. Keep up-to-date on the latest art news and listings at pimpguides.com

Q: What's the weirdest thing that's happened to you in London?

"Liam Gallagher signed one of my paintings at the Pimp exhibition in Covent Garden while I was not there." →

Elms Lesters Painting Rooms

1-3-5 Flitcroft Street, WC2H 8DH
020 7836 6747
www.elmslesters.co.uk
Tube: Tottenham Court Road
Open: Tue-Sat 12:00-18:00, Thu 12:00-21:00

Tucked away in an alley at the back of Centre Point, Elms Lesters Painting Rooms is a hidden gem in the truest sense. While it was purpose built in 1904 for scenic painting, a tradition that continues to this day, it's found a nice sideline showcasing work from the world's finest counter-culture and urban artists. In fact, from Kaws, Futura and Stash to Ron English, Delta, Anthony Lister and Adam Neate, the gallery offers a rare chance to see the glitterati of this movement. Its unusual location also means that often you'll get to enjoy them pretty much on your own.

053

ICA

054

12 Carlton House Terrace, SW1Y 5AH
020 7930 3647
www.ica.org.uk
Tube: Charing Cross
Open: Mon 12:00-23:00, Tue-Sat 12:00-01:00, Sun 12:00-22:30

One of the most respected contemporary art centres in the world, the Institute of Contemporary Arts (ICA) is a playground for artists whose work offers an innovative look at today's culture. Situated within an impressive structure on The Mall, the ICA exhibits world cinema, art, theatre and new media, and hosts educational speakers, and club nights. Film is represented in two theatres, each screening documentaries and shorts from around the world. You'll find an excellent arts programme along with live performances by the capital's best new alternative musicians. The ICA bar excels in its own right, hosting club nights and regular parties. The ICA also boasts a brilliant little on-site bookshop.

Q: WHERE'S YOUR FAVOURITE PLACE TO GO FOR A DRINK?

"Anywhere that doesn't sell saussison [sic] and pomme de terre for £22.58. Or swordfish. Or eggs Benedict — it's a pub not a restaurant and I want a pint. I love finding old Victorian pubs down the backstreets, the ones with tiled walls that smell of real ale. I don't like the ones that think they are cool by taking over old shoe shops and leaving them half finished to adopt the squat look, with DJs that play wedding disco music from their iPods because they think it's hip. It's shit and it gives you a hangover before you leave. And you wake up in the morning in some silly drama student's bed."

Lazarides 055

8 Greek Street, W1D 4DG
020 3214 0055
www.lazinc.com
Tube: Tottenham Court Road
Open: Tue-Sat 11:00-19:00

Lazarides boasts an impressive stable of cult artists in the capital; exclusively representing the UK's most infamous graffiti artist, Banksy. Pioneering the underground art movement's development in a notoriously elitist art industry, Lazarides exhibits one of the greatest collections of urban art in London, with shows by Mode2, Faile, Invader, David Choe, Paul Insect, Antony Micallef and, of course, Banksy. A fantastic gallery, this space is highly recommended for those interested in subversive art. If your budget doesn't extend to the works on sale here, head over to the Lazarides Print Shop, which sells prints, drawings, books and toys by the artists represented here. Lazarides **Print Shop:** 1st Floor, 125 Charing Cross Road, WC2H 0EW. T: 020 3238 0108. Tube: Tottenham Court Road

01 Antony Micallef *'Peace keeper',* 2006
Oil on canvas
115cm x 140cm
Image courtesy of the artist and Lazarides Gallery. ©Antony Micallef, 2008

02 Lazarides Gallery exhibition: Faile, *From Brooklyn With Love,* March/April 2007. Image courtesy of Lazarides Gallery. ©Lazarides Gallery, 2008

03 Paul Insect *'Dance Boy',* 2007
Acrylic & Emulsion on wood panel
Image courtesy of Lazarides Gallery. ©Paul Insect, 2008

04 Ben Turnbull *'Bring me the Head of Saddam Hussein',* 2008
Mixed media, acrylic and spray paint
7 x 5 x 4 ft
Image courtesy of the artist and Lazarides Gallery. ©Ben Turnbull, 2008

Proud 056

5 Buckingham Street, WC2N 6BP
020 7839 4942
www.proud.co.uk
Tube: Covent Garden
Open: Mon-Sat 11:00-19:00, Sun 11:00-18:00

Photography gallery, Proud is famous for its exhibitions of pop culture works: *Destroy: The Sex Pistols, Rankin's Nudes,* and *Hip Hop Immortals* have all shown here, which has ensured the venue popularity with the more cultured segment of London's youth market. A mixed clientele of celebrities, and fans of music, politics, fashion and film visit either this venue, or the infamous sister gallery over in Camden, which doubles as a live music venue.

Gallery **Maison Bertaux**

28 Greek Street, W1D 5DQ. T: 07985 395079. Tube: Leicester Square. Open: Mon-Fri 08:30-23:00, Sun 09:30-20:00

Situated above a Soho patisserie of the same name, Gallery Maison Bertaux is a brilliant little art space for investing in off-the-wall artwork. Founder, Tania Wade, represents the art of *The Mighty Boosh* comedian, Noel Fielding, who had his first solo show at the gallery recently. Under the auspices of Wade, both Fielding and the gallery are making a big impact on London's art scene. At the time of writing, Wade is planning a collaborative exhibition between the artist and rock and roll photographer, Nobby Clark. Obviously, having these high-profile names on board ensures a steady influx of major stars to the space, making it one of the most exciting galleries in London right now.

The Amuti Gallery

10 Woburn Walk, WC1H 0JL. T: 020 7387 8417
W: www.amutionline.com Tube: Euston. Open: Wed-Thu 11:00-18:00, Fri 11:00-20:00, Sat 12:00-17:00

The Amuti is brought to us by the founders of the Aquarium gallery over in Farringdon, which works with reactionary artists like godfather of punk, Jamie Reid. This gallery and bookshop deals in art, fashion, books and collectables by the artists who exhibit at the gallery including James Cauty and Billy Childish. Rare books (including first editions), punk tees by John Dove and Molly White (they kitted out the Sex Pistols back in the day), comics, journals plus artworks are all on sale here. Art exhibitions also feature regularly.

Frith Street Gallery

17-18 Golden Square, W1F 9JJ
T: 020 7494 1550. W: www.frithstreetgallery.com
Tube: Piccadilly Circus. Open: Tue-Fri 10:00-18:00, Sat 11:00-17:00

Frith Street Gallery exhibits UK and international contemporary artists working in painting, photography, sculpture and film.

Gallery Maison Bertaux

See the gallery review above.

The Gallery Soho

125 Charing Cross Road, WC2H 0EW. T: 020 7287 1779. Tube: Tottenham Court Road
Open: Times vary

The Gallery Soho is a dynamic four-floor contemporary art gallery/workspace with a regularly changing events programme. In addition to art
and photography exhibitions, you'll find independent fashion and photography bookshop, Claire de Rouen Books, and the Lazarides Print Shop.

The Horse Hospital

30 Colonnade, WC1N 1JD. T: 020 7833 3644
W: www.thehorsehospital.com Tube: Russell Square
Open: Times vary

This arts space is a must-visit for fans of rare avant-garde. Spanning three decades of pop culture, The Horse Hospital offers a targeted programme of underground film, art, culture and performance, in addition to external events by book publishers, fashion colleges and record labels.

Nancy Victor Gallery

Basement, 36 Charlotte Street, W1T 2NJ
T: 020 7813 0373. W: www.nancyvictor.com
Tube: Goodge Street. Open: Mon-Fri 10:00-18:00

Home to artists such as Remi/Rough and Juice 126, the Nancy Victor gallery is an artist-run space showcasing urban art.

The National Gallery

Trafalgar Square, WC2N 5DN. T: 020 7747 2885
W: www.nationalgallery.org.uk Tube: Charing Cross
Open: Daily 10:00-18:00, Wed 10:00-21:00

Epic overseer of Trafalgar Square with an exuberant love of Western European art circa 1250-1900, n/s, gsoh seeks van Gogh, da Vinci and Michelangelo aficionado, male or female, age/looks unimportant, preferably n/s for fun, friendship, possibly more. No charge for the pleasure. Voicebox 07564.

The Photographers' Gallery

5 & 8 Great Newport Street, WC2H 7HY. T: 020 7831 1772
W: www.photonet.org.uk Tube: Leicester Square
Open: Mon-Sat 11:00-18:00, Thu 11:00-20:00, Sun 12:00-18:00

An independent contemporary photography gallery
introducing new and major names in the field including
André Kertesz and Irving Penn.

Tate Britain

Millbank, SW1P 4RG. T: 020 7887 8888
W: www.tate.org.uk Tube: Pimlico. Open: Daily 10:00–17:30

Tate Britain is London's most famous art gallery, hous-
ing the largest collection of British art from the 1500s to
present. The Tate is behind the prestigious Turner Prize,
so you can expect to see current and previous winners
here, alongside the Old Masters, Pre-Raphaelite paintings and contemporary works by world-leading artists
like Henry Moore and Francis Bacon. It has also unwittingly exhibited the work of Banksy who famously
added one of his own paintings to the Tate collection. He
smuggled his art into the gallery where it sat unnoticed
until it fell off the wall a few hours later. It's not the first
time the Tate has been hit by the artist; he also painted
'Mind the Crap' on its steps, ahead of the Turner Prize
award ceremony. Late at Tate Britain (on the first Friday
of each month) plays host to exhibitions, music, talks, performance and film.

Tate Modern

Bankside, SE1 9TG. T: 020 7887 8888. W: www.tate.org.uk/modern
Tube: Southwark. Open: Sun-Thu 10:00-18:00, Fri & Sat 10:00-22:00

The younger sibling of the Tate Britain, this converted pow-
erstation exhibits contemporary and modern art from 1900
onwards. Appealing to young and old art fans alike, the Tate
Modern is the best in the capital for modern art movements
including Surrealism, Fauvism and Pop Art. Many of the greatest paintings in the world hang here with works on show by
Warhol, Dali, Pollock, Matisse, Picasso and many more. Its
conceptual art programme lends itself to innovative new art
exhibitions, including Doris Salcedo's now infamous installation which created a 548-ft crack in the floor.

CARRI (CASSETTE PLAYA)

Q: Someone arrives in London for only 4 hours and you are their guide. Where do you take them? "Trocadero, to eat sweets'n play computer games." Q: Where's your first stop when shopping for clothes? "I shop in Kokon to Zai, Goodhood, The Hideout, Dalston market and Primark." Q: Best places to buy music? "Rough Trade (Acklam Road) / Rhythm Division (Bow)."

DJ/Fashion Designer

Photography by Keex

North

You used to get lots of people saying things like 'north London would kick south London's ass' or 'the sexy south ain't got nothing on the **naughty** north' but these days people are smart enough to know that comments like that make them sound retarded. Sure, you get some kids settling their North/South differences with guns the same size as that midget from *Austin Powers*, but they're **gang members,** so you'd kind of expect that type of behaviour. Most people are more concerned with heading down to Camden to see the next **Pete Doherty** or Johnny Borrell. Well, at least they used to be. There was a time when drug addiction and arrogance made the rock star, and the **Camden Barfly** has definitely witnessed its fair share of cocky trilby-wearing poets and pasty-faced **junkies.** But once the kids realised that The Libertines would never reform, they soon got bored and moved down the road to **Koko,** the former Camden Palace. Like a bigger, cleaner and meaner Barfly, the Koko nightclub has been overrun by teeny boppers desperate for their latest fix of **NME-endorsed hype.** But, let's jump out of the hustle and bustle of Camden for a second and visit the leafy surroundings of East Finchley's Bishops Avenue, where you get to see your own episode of **MTV *Cribs*** up close and personal. Nicknamed 'Millionaires' Row' by many, the smallest house costs like **3 million pounds** and Arab princes often recreate *Saturday Night Fever* in their bedrooms. Your invite is most certainly not in the post.

For decades, north London has witnessed legendary performances by the greatest names in music. Whether cutting their teeth at a grubby little boozer or playing for mass audiences via televised gigs at Koko, bands perform in north London's neighbourhoods every night of the week. Home to every genre of music known to man, this area offers more gig spots than any other part of London.

Joana and the Wolf at The Dublin Castle; photography by Garysh Productions

BARFLY

9 Chalk Farm Road, NW1 8AN. T: 020 7424 0800. W: www.barflyclub.com Tube: Chalk Farm. Open: Times vary   00

This infamous live music venue has been a haunt for music fans and excitable indie-kids since before the Britpop era, throughout The Strokes' overtake of London town, and up until the present day. Pretty much anyone who's anyone has played here, and it's now a benchmark gigging spot for budding musicians.

The Buffalo Bar   002

59 Upper Street, N1 1RU (The basement of the Famous Cock Tavern)
020 7359 6191
www.buffalobar.co.uk
Tube: Highbury & Islington
Open: Times vary

Highbury's Buffalo Bar is an underground alt-rock den with live bands playing most nights of the week. Predominantly an indie-rock and punk venue, the Buffalo plays a crucial role in pushing good music in the area. Acts like Bloc Party took to Buffalo's stage in their early career and the 150-capacity venue continues to lend itself as a platform for emerging talent. Club nights worth a visit include *artrocker* magazine's Tuesday night residency, which introduces many of the bands that grace its pages.

THE
DUBLIN
CASTLE   00

94 Parkway, NW1 7AN
020 7485 1773
www.thedublincastle.com
Tube: Camden Town
Open: Mon-Thu 12:00-00:00, Fri-Sun 12:00-02:00

The original and still one of the best, The Dublin Castle manages to succeed where so many others have failed. Oozing character, the venue is, and always will be, painfully rock and roll with posters and music memorabilia plastered across every wall (including the landlord's own signed collection of Madness singles). Its daytime audience is a slightly older crowd, but at night, this place comes alive. A hangout for band members, The Dublin Castle is a fantastically intimate venue, with the stage area at the back creating just the right ambience for both lighter and thrashier styles of music. It's always packed, so get here early to enjoy the authenticity of Camden's flagship indie venue.

CSS concert at Koko; photography by Che Blomfield, see page 114

The Enterprise

004

Haverstock Hill, NW3 2BL
20 7485 2659
ube: Chalk Farm
Open: Mon-Sat 11:00-23:00, Sun 12:00-22:30

Minding its own at the north-end of Chalk Farm Road, The Enterprise is an old-school pub/club, gnarled by years of abuse at the hands of numerous promoters and bands. Most notably, it was the venue for Alan McGee's Creation Records) legendary Living Room Club in the mid-eighties, where the world was first introduced to acts such as Primal Scream and The Jesus and Mary Chain. Despite such lofty musical history, there's a down-to-earth charm to this place, reflected in the lack of pretension and broad mix of punters. Everything about the pub is straightforward: good beers on tap, great food, both reasonably priced. We especially love the back room with its open fire and bookcases; it has that great lived-in feel, perfect for relaxing afternoon sessions.

The Good Mixer

005

0 Inverness Street, NW1 7HJ
20 7916 6176
ube: Camden Town
Open: Mon-Sun 11:00-23:00

You just can't help but love this pub. Occupying a space somewhere between a working men's club and a scout hut serving alcohol, its interior is unique to say the least. With kitsch tongue and groove panelling and a peculiar split bar room layout, design-wise this place shouldn't really work, yet somehow it does. It's all about atmos-phere, you see. An expertly-filled rock and roll jukebox provides the music, while local misfits and Camden characters provide the entertainment. A famous hang-out for bands of the Britpop era — due to its proximity to the then neighbouring Food Records — the pub still smacks of 'cool Britannia' today, being frequented by bands of the moment, as well as a few casualties from back then. As important to Camden as the market, you should definitely stop in for a beer if you find yourself in this part of town.

THE HOPE AND ANCHOR

00

07 Upper Street, N1 1RL
020 7354 1312
Tube: Highbury and Islington
Open: Mon-Wed 12:00-23:00, Thu-Sat 12:00-01:00, Sun 12:00-22:30

You wouldn't know to look at it, but this place is drippin in rock and roll history. The Hope and Anchor is one o London's most famous live music pubs. Don't let the rathe unremarkable main bar throw you; if you look, you wi find a few signs of the pub's musical history dotted aroun — mainly band photos and other bits of memorabilia Downstairs, however, is a different story. Unchanged fo over thirty years, bands still play the same suffocating dark, beer cellar: the likes of the Sex Pistols, The Stranglers Elvis Costello, Joy Division and more recently, The Lib ertines played early shows here. The importance of thi place in London's musical fabric is way beyond the scop of this review, but with new and established bands playin every night of the week, don't just take our word for it, g see and feel it for yourself.

SINGER / SONGWRITER

AKIKO

Q: Where's your favourite place to go for a drink? "A pub called The Dolphin in Hackney stays open till really late, I quite like it there."
Q: Where's your first stop when shopping for clothes? "Bands' merchandise tables from venues. You can find good designs of T-shirts, badges, bags, bandanas — you can only get them at their shows usually. Good bands usually know good illustrators and designers who do their artwork. I would never wear it if the band is shit, even the design is good, though. I always wait till I watch the band before buying their merch. Also, I like Hoxton Boutique & no-one in Old Street."

KOKO

007

1A Camden High Street, NW1 7JE
020 7388 3222
www.koko.uk.com
Tube: Mornington Crescent
Open: Times vary. Doors open at 19:00

Formerly the Camden Palace, Koko is a music landmark not only of London, but the entire country. After a bout of serious restoration in 2004, Koko emerged an indie-institution; integral on any touring band's venue list, such is its importance to the capital's music scene. Packed to the hilt on any given night, the opulent, Victoriana-meets-art-deco interior is home to some huge club nights including the NME's weekly extravaganza which attracts indie-kids in their binge-drinking droves. But, it's not all spotty teens with Pete Doherty complexes. As a gig venue, Koko's theatrical heritage (balconies and boxes intact) offers an astonishing live music experience you rarely find these days. If the opportunity arises to see a band you love play here, take it.

CSS concert at Koko; photography by Che Blomfield

The Lock Tavern

008

5 Chalk Farm Road, NW1 8AJ
www.lock-tavern.co.uk
020 7482 7163
Tube: Camden Town or Chalk Farm
Open: Mon-Thu 12:00-00:00, Fri-Sat 12:00-01:00, Sun 12:00-23:00

It's always raining in Camden. Whatever the season, you're guaranteed it'll be pissing down in NW1. Once those grey skies open up, it's time to leave the Stables and head to the Lock Tavern. A self-described 'tarted-up boozer' the LT is a warm and welcoming solace down the lowly stretch of Chalk Farm Road. Renowned for its ace music policy, comfort food and attracting Camden's indie royalty, this pub has an unpretentious, low-key party vibe that gets pretty crazy in the evenings. And if on that rare occasion the sun smiles, there's a beer garden and roof terrace to enjoy. *We also recommend the Lock Tavern's sister pub, the Amersham Arms, over in New Cross. See page 128*

Nambucca

010

96 Holloway Road, N7 6LB
020 7272 7366
www.myspace.com/nambucca
Tube: Holloway Road
Open: Daily 13:00-late

With so many new UK bands first tasting success on the Nambucca stage, this pub-club has built a deserved reputation as one of the best neighbourhood music venues in London. With bands four nights a week and one of the most popular indie-club nights around, Nambucca draws music lovers from across the city. There's an incredibly relaxed and friendly atmosphere here, which is all too rare in pubs populated by London's indie-elite. But, be warned, this is one of those places where you can easily find yourself sitting opposite your favourite band. Speaking from experience, there's nothing worse than waking up and remembering you had a lead singer in a drunken headlock, while telling him to sack his guitarist and hire you instead. We recommend an air of nonchalant indifference at all times. Keep this in mind and you'll be fine.

The Luminaire

009

311 High Road, Kilburn, NW6 7JR
020 7372 7123
www.theluminaire.co.uk
Tube: Kilburn
Open: Sun-Wed 19:30-00.00, Thu 19:30-01.00, Fri & Sat 19:30-02.00

This live music venue is one of the capital's finest, with several awards to prove it. It's a favourite destination of music fans, who are attracted to the calibre of the acts who play here: Hot Chip, Babyshambles and Datarock, to name a few. Considerably more attractive than the usual dirty holes that typify London's live music scene, its retro design and 250-capacity make for an intimate gig experience. In addition to the live music upstairs, there's a bar and kitchen downstairs with plenty of comfy sofas and booths.

The Roundhouse

01

Chalk Farm Road, NW1 8EH
0844 482 8008
www.roundhouse.org.uk
Tube: Chalk Farm
Open: Performance times vary

The Roundhouse is a legendary music venue in Camden which has seen performances by eminent acts including Jimi Hendrix, the Rolling Stones and The Doors. It has housed countless illustrious gigs since it first opened its doors as an arts venue in 1964. The Roundhouse is no less popular today. The Grade II-listed site underwent a multi-million pound redevelopment in 2004 and reopened as a 3000-capacity creative centre and performance space, continuing its reputation for hosting great music, theatre, film and digital media events.

The Scala   012

275 Pentonville Road, N1 9NL
020 7833 2022
W: www.scala-london.co.uk
Tube: King's Cross
Open: Times Vary

The Scala boasts underground gigs, industry showcases and an eclectic club night policy. The grand old theatre's striking marble-led 1920s decor, excellent sound system and unique layout make it a popular club, but due to the 980-capacity and huge main room, the venue's got to be pretty busy to generate enough buzz to flow through its three bars and two dance floors. That said, a line-up of the best rising and world-leading musicians often guarantees sell-out shows.

The Water Rats   013

328 Grays Inn Road, WC1X 8BZ
020 7837 4412
www.themonto.com
Open: Times vary. Doors normally open at 19:00
Tube: King's Cross

The Water Rats is one of London's longstanding live music venues and an essential spot on London's band circuit. Packed with A&R men looking for the next big thing, this place has seen early performances from most of the major acts and continues to play host to exciting breakthrough artists.

All You Can Eat at Electrowerkz, photography by Billa, see page 119

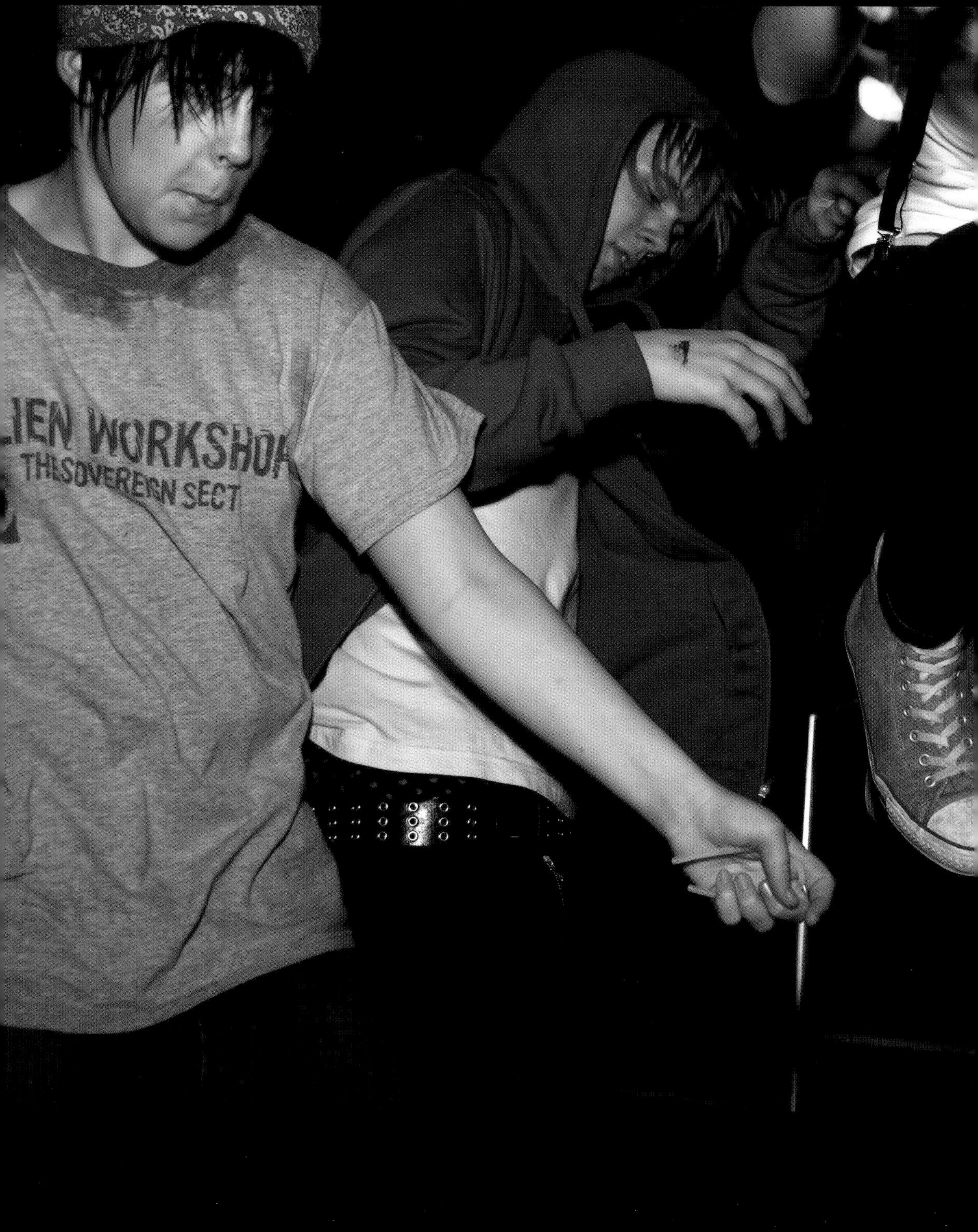
THESOVEREIGN SECT

atProud

The Horse Hospital, The Stables Market, Chalk Farm Road, NW1 8AH. T: 020 7482 3867
W: www.atproud.com Tube: Chalk Farm
Open: Performance times vary

atProud is the best hybrid venue in this neighbourhood, with three rooms dedicated to art and photography exhibitions and live music. For full review, see page 125.

Bull & Gate

389 Kentish Town, NW5 2TJ. T: 020 8826 5000
W: www.bullandgate.co.uk Tube: Kentish Town
Open: Daily 11:00-23:00

Overshadowed by The Forum next door, the Bull and Gate is a pub/live music venue, mainly hosting local bands including the occasional gem. It does have a certain charm so it's worth dropping by if you're in this neck of the woods.

EGG

200 York Way, N7 9AP. T: 020 7609 8364
W: www.egglondon.net Tube: King's Cross
Open: Times vary

The King's Cross weekend-only super club, Egg, has a music policy spanning electro, deep house and old school classics. In addition to externally-hosted parties by Horsemeat Disco and Disco Bloodbath, the Friday club night, Alwayz Frydaze, is the Egg gig worthy of your attention, having previously featured Wet Yourself, Boy Better Know, and Redlight DJs. Here, club-goers party hard across the venue's four dance arenas until Sunday afternoon close. Check what's on before heading down so there are no unpleasant surprises.

Electrowerkz

7 Torrens Street, EC1V 1NQ. T: 020 7837 6419
W: www.electrowerkz.com Tube: Angel
Open: Times vary

This dingy warehouse venue is used by promoters for parties like club-kid favourite, All You Can Eat. Each promoter attracts a different audience so check listings first.

The Scala photography by Grace Pattison, see page 117

The Forum

9-17 Highgate Road, NW5 1JY. T: 0844 847 2405. W: www.kentishtownforum.com Tube: Kentish Town. Open: Times vary

Standing at 2000-capacity, The Forum attracts crowd-pulling acts who, to date, include Prince, Velvet Underground, Oasis and James Brown. Recent performances by Pete Doherty, The Horrors and De La Soul reflect the diversity of this place's music policy.

Carling Academy Islington

N1 Centre, 16 Parkfield Street, N1 0PS. T: 0844 477 2000 (24 hrs). W: www.islington-academy.co.uk Tube: Angel. Open: Times vary

Islington Academy is one of the major live music venues in London, attracting internationally-acclaimed acts. Sister to the Brixton Academy, this site is home to concerts, Xfm's regular live sessions and MTV music gigs. The adjoining Bar Academy is a smaller, stand-alone gig venue dedicated to new talent. Call ahead, or visit the website for advance gig listings.

The Good Ship

289 Kilburn High Road, NW6 7JR. W: www.the-goodship.co.uk Tube: Kilburn. Open: Mon-Thu & Sun till 02:00, Fri-Sat till 04:00

A live music/club/arts centre showcasing new band talent. Punters will also enjoy a varied programme of film and stand up comedy.

Jazz Cafe

5 Parkway, Camden, NW1 7PG. T: 020 7916 6060 W: www.jazzcafelive.com Tube: Camden Town Open: Mon-Sun 19:00-02:00

The Jazz Cafe is an institution for soul, jazz and funk. An up-close and personal, but always electric live experience, the list of legendary soul sisters and funkateers who have got on the good foot here is unbelievable: Gil Scott-Heron, Roy Ayers, Lyn Collins, Gwen McCrae, Mos Def, to name but a few. A dining balcony overlooks the stage where tables can be reserved to enjoy the show from a less sweaty vantage point. Reasonable drink prices, a constant flow of quality music and a laid back, good-time crowd mean a visit to Camden is imminent.

The Old Queen's Head

44 Essex Road N1 8LN. T: 020 7354 9993 W: www.theoldqueenshead.com Tube: Angel Open: Mon-Wed & Sun 12:00-00:00, Thu 12:00-01:00, Fri & Sat 12:00-02:00

If you're out and about in Islington and fancy a pint, The Old Queen's Head is one of the nicest (and oldest) boozers in this area. Within the vast but cosily-designed bar (complete with open fireplace and leather sofas), you can relax among a crowd of local urbanites. Midweek, the entertainment policy moves between acoustic performances, poetry readings, music quizzes and cabaret. At the weekend, promoters take over the upstairs area, and Sunday lunches are accompanied by DJ sets.

The Westbury

34 Kilburn High Road, NW6 5UA. T: 020 7625 7500 W: www.westburybar.com Tube: Kilburn Open: Mon-Wed 12:00-00:00, Thu 12:00-01:00 Fri & Sat 12:00-03:00, Sun 12:00-23:00

This little boozer sees acts like Hot Chip, Ed Simons (Chemical brothers), Bugz in the Attic and Sir Norman Jay take to its decks. Sister venue to The Old Queen's Head in Islington, The Westbury holds regular parties for its mixed clientele.

The Forum photograph by Lucia Graca

162 (21st Century Retro)

014

162 Holloway Road, N7 8DD. T: 020 7700 2354. Tube: Holloway Road. Open: Mon-Sat 10:00-18:00, Sun 11:00-18:00

This fantastic vintage clothing emporium is off the beaten track so it's still relatively unknown to most Londoners. But for stylists, fashion students and north London locals, 162 affords them exclusive enjoyment of over 6000 vintage garments from the US and Europe, all at ridiculously low prices (dresses and jackets cost from as little as £3). New stock from the 1940s to 2000s arrives regularly and you'll find designer, high street, little-known and defunct labels covering everything from period to contemporary fashion.

all week anyway. You stand a much better chance of rummaging for bargains when you're not fighting against a swarm of despondent, suburban Goth kids, whose only purpose seems to be looking miserable and getting in your way. Go in the week, they're at school, and you can have the place pretty much to yourself. Unless you're a Goth kid, then we'd advise the weekend; have a ball, get something pierced, we don't care, just get out of our way.

Arckiv Eyewear

015

Unit 87, Stables Market, Chalk Farm Road, NW1 8AH
07790 102 204
Tube: Chalk Farm
Open: Tue-Fri 13:00-18:00, Sat-Sun 10:00-18:00

When you spot great sunglasses on the most stylish young heads in London, chances are, they were purchased at Arckiv Eyewear. Word-of-mouth buzz spread like wildfire upon this store's opening, with the fashion pack flocking to the space in their droves to grab a pair of rare frames and one-of-a-kind vintage prototypes. Founder, Fraser Laing has amassed an awesome collection of glasses for this store and even supplies and develops eyewear for major film releases, worn by actors like Johnny Depp. His self-professed "detective work" in unearthing unique eyewear married with his historical knowledge, makes Arckiv much more than just a shop; you're guaranteed to find the most fashionable sunglasses in town. *The shop fits lenses for £25 or if you want to design your own eyewear, Arckiv will make them for you.*

Haggle Vinyl **018**

114-116 Essex Road, N1 8LX
020 7704 3101
www.flashback.co.uk
Tube: Angel
Open: Mon-Sat 09:00-19:00, Sun 09:30-16:00

For those with a serious vinyl itch, Haggle Vinyl is as good a backscratcher as any. The window promises 50 years of music and 50 years of hoarding is what you get. Watched over by pin-up obscurities on the walls, boxes of vinyl fall over each other spewing music of all persuasions. Good for everything from bagpipe soul jazz or Swedish rockabilly to white labels pressed when hardcore was at its zenith. Just don't expect any bargains unless you've got all day and a need to get a little dusty.

Camden Stables Market

016

Chalk Farm Road, NW1 8AH
Tube: Chalk Farm
Open: Daily 10:00-18:00

At the time of writing, Camden's famous Stables Market is undergoing redevelopment — a few cosmetic tweaks here and there, in order to drag it into the 21st century. So, depending on the time you visit, there may be a little less or more going on than usual. The markets in Camden are world famous; apparently they rate fourth on the most popular tourist attractions list. 'Tourist attraction', translation: 100,000 people squeezed into Camden's tiny streets every weekend, making for some pretty hectic, and if we do say so, annoying crowds. While some of the 500-odd stalls might be closed weekdays, we still advise you take the opportunity to visit during this time. The really good stores (vintage clothes, records, sneakers), pubs and bars are open

Opposite: Flashback and Labour of Love photography by Keex

FLASHBACK

017

50 Essex Road, N1 8LR. T: 020 7354 9356. W: www.flashback.co.uk Tube: Angel. Open: Mon-Sat 10:00-19:00, Sun 12:00-18:00

Flashback specialises in second-hand vinyl and CDs, with a comprehensive selection of genres spanning four decades. In the basement, you'll find albums, 7" and 12"s, with everything from hip hop bangers, classic soul, rock and blues to film soundtracks, all waiting for someone to lend them an ear. Best of all is the pricing. Flashback is considerably cheaper than most second-hand record stores, even for rarities. So if you're a collector or simply want some music for a house party, you can be sure to bag a bargain here. Flashback also sells old cassettes and VHS videos plus games and DVDs.

Know How Records

019

3 Buck Street, NW1 8NJ
020 7267 1526
www.knowhowrecords.co.uk
Tube: Camden Town
Open: Mon-Sat 11:00-19:00, Sun 12:00-18:00

Home to breaks label, Audio Bug, Know How Records is renowned for its great selection of music, and for always having the latest promos and imports. The store invites you in before you've even reached Buck Street with music pumping into the street till closing. Know How stocks just about every sub-genre of break beat you can think of, and you can expect to see bassline, old skool classics, drum 'n' bass and breaks lining the walls. Other musical tastes are catered for as well, and various accessories including slip mats and record bags are on sale.

Labour of Love

020

193 Upper Street, N1 1RQ
020 7354 9333
www.labour-of-love.co.uk
Tube: Highbury & Islington
Open: Mon-Wed, Fri & Sat 11:00-18:30, Thu 11:00-19:00, Sun 12:30-17:30

This womenswear boutique stands head and shoulders above the rest in this area. Shunning brand marketing hype, Labour of Love has solely relied on word-of-mouth to propel it to success, and it is now a sought-after fashion destination. You won't find rails of factory-produced designer garbs here; instead a hand-picked selection of garments and accessories by embryonic European labels, many of which are stocked here exclusively. The boutique's founder, Francesca, has a keen eye for talent so not only will you pick up rare clothing, jewellery, shoes and homeware, but you'll also be one of the first to own product by the rising names in fashion.

PALETTE

021

21 Canonbury Lane, N1 2AS
020 7288 7428
W: www.palette-london.com
Tube: Highbury & Islington
Open: Mon-Wed, Fri & Sat 11:00-18:30, Thu 11:00-19:00, Sun 12:00-17:30

Palette is a high-end vintage design store specialising in clothing, accessories, homeware and art from the 1940s-1980s. Every item on sale in this Islington boutique is in mint condition and although prices start from £10, they can easily reach hundreds of pounds thanks to rare stock by Oscar de la Renta, Chanel, Pucci and Diane Von Furstenberg. There's an extensive collection of handbags (£15+) and shoes (£40+) by Hermes, Gucci and Fendi in addition to jewellery (from the 1920s+), furniture, books & mags and lingerie. Look out for the vintage Betsey Johnson and 1980s designs by Comme des Garçons.

SOUND 323

023

323 Archway Road, N6 5AA
020 8348 9595
www.sound323.com
Tube: Highgate
Open: Tue–Sat 12:00-17:30

Nestled in the leafy suburb of Highgate, Sound 323/Second Layer Records (located in the basement of the former), is one of the capital's best kept secrets — until now. Specialising in 'fringe music', these two conjoined record stores carry an amazing range of sonic obscurities, DVDs, books and peripheral publications. From experimental, noise, electronica,

Pure Groove

022

679 Holloway Road, N19 5SE
020 7281 4877
www.puregroove.co.uk
Tube: Archway
Open: Mon-Wed, Fri & Sat 10:00-18:00, Thu 11:00-19:00

Highly respected independent record store and label, Pure Groove is north London's best music retailer, bar none. Crate diggers hunting vintage vinyl may want to stay with more central stores, as these guys deal in only now-sounds. Not that this is a problem; the store is very much an all-killer, no-filler kind of establishment, covering the genre spectrum. Playing host to in-store record launches, you'll find a regular line-up of the best emerging bands and artists performing here, and it's also a fantastic source for the plethora of underground 'zines and alternative publications circulating in the capital.

At the time of writing, our beloved Pure Groove is preparing an imminent move to larger, sexier premises in east London, so you will need to check the website for details. They've promised us it's going to be bloody marvellous, so check it out.

Pure Groove: 6-7 West Smithfield, EC1A 9JX. Tube: Farringdon

avant-rock, free-jazz, improv, dub, psychedelia and krautrock, it's a music geek's wet dream, and we love it. Owned and run by music obsessives, for music obsessives, there's more cool music squeezed into this tiny double-decker store than all the HMVs in London. It's a pilgrimage well worth taking for anyone interested in (proper) underground music.

Pure Groove photography by Kee*

Sound 323 photograph courtesy of Sound 323

atProud

The Horse Hospital, Stables Market, Chalk Farm Road, NW1 8AH
020 7482 3867
www.atproud.com
Tube: Camden Town or Chalk Farm
Open: Mon-Thu 10:00-01:30, Fri-Sat 10:00-02:30, Sun 10:00-00:00

The star of north London's art scene, atProud is the best hybrid venue in this neighbourhood for rock 'n' roll parties, live music, and art and photography exhibitions. Having recently relocated to a bigger and better location at The Horse Hospital in the Stables Market, atProud exhibits an unrivalled collection of pop culture works. Celebrities, indie-kids and culture aficionados are its clientele, keen to view the latest works by infamous artists and photographers like subway art documenter, Martha Cooper. atProud presents live music most nights of the week, and promoters regularly drop by to host parties and exhibitions in the three rooms and outside terrace (complete with deckchairs adorned with the faces of rock 'n' roll stars). Possibly the first gallery to become a legend in its infancy.

atProud photography by Ben Speck

Sadler's Wells Theatre

Rosebery Avenue, EC1R 4TN. T: 0844 412 4300. W: www.sadlerswells.com
Tube: Angel. Open: Performance times vary

Sadler's Wells has been offering contemporary dance events in London for over 300 years. From the ballet reworking of *Edward Scissorhands* to the hip hop version of *One Flew Over the Cuckoo's Nest*, this theatre has long sat at the cutting edge of the arts. Its celebration of all styles of dance extends to street culture when the three-day international hip hop festival, the Breakin' Convention takes over. Curated by Sadler's Wells associate artist, Jonzi D, this annual event features the finest b-boys and girls from across the globe along with a programme of classic hip hop documentaries, Q&As with pioneers of the movement, and art & photography exhibitions.

Victoria Miro Gallery

16 Wharf Road, N1 7RW. T: 020 7336 8109. W: www.victoria-miro.com
Tube: Angel. Open: Tue-Sat 10:00-18:00

One of London's largest commercial art galleries, Victoria Miro is home to a wealth of talent including Turner Prize winners Chris Ofili and Grayson Perry, and nominees: Ian Hamilton Finlay, Peter Doig, Isaac Julien and Phil Collins.

THE REAL HEAT

Where's your favourite place to eat out in London?
ZAZA: Coming back from a club in the West End, there's nothing like a Duck and Noodle soup from The Mayflower in Soho to get rid of any potential hangovers.
SUKI: And there's a Vietnamese restaurant on Kingsland Road which is really good. They let you bring in your own alcohol too.
SHAKI: Ecco's Italian restaurant in Clapham do the best calzone ever.

Where's your favourite place to go for a drink?
ZAZA: I go to a pub in Pimlico called The William. I call it 'the place that time forgot' because it's so eerie; it's really something! If you went there, you'd know what I mean.

Where's your first stop when shopping for clothes?
SUKI: Camden and east London have to be the two most vibrant areas fashion-wise. I go to the boutiques on Brick Lane and Camden Market. Portobelllo on a Saturday is good too.
SHAKI: I like to buy my clothes from second-hand shops like TRAID, specialist boutiques like Joy or Laden Showrooms and sports shops like JD Sports. The rest is top secret.

Best place to see live music?
ZAZA: Tube buskers are highly recommended. There's a lady that plays the comb outside Brixton tube station and her outfits are crazy colourful.
SUKI: Yeah, she wears giant earrings and Nigerian head-gear with flowers and things hanging off it, and massive bag lady gowns. She's quite a character.
SHAKI: 93 Feet East, Bar Music Hall (Shoreditch); Amersham Arms (New Cross); Madame JoJo's (Soho).

Favourite club(s) / nights?
SHAKI: My favorite club is Hannah Holland's Trailer Trash party.
SUKI: Bar Music Hall — it has a really nice atmosphere. It's non-stop party music so you just dance all night! And Nuke 'Em All is the party of all parties right now.

Photography by Rick Pushinsky

South

Kele Okereke is an enigma. A rock star of **African descent,** who doesn't look like he sprinkles coke on his Shredded Wheat of a morning. Kele and his band Bloc Party were part of the imaginatively titled **'New Cross Scene'.** There were a few other bands involved in the movement, but they don't really matter. They say that 'New York is the big city of dreams', but if you want that new, raw uncut shit, then it's all about New Cross. Birthplace of **Klaxons** and cheap chicken shops, the streets are paved with students and although the slogan 'Student Life Rules, OK' sounds like something **Harry Potter** would tattoo on his arm, life at **Goldsmiths** university has so much more to offer than a 2:1 and shitty food. With glorious ex-students such as Damien Hirst and the creator of hot pants, Mary Quant, Goldsmiths is just a stone's throw away from the **Amersham Arms** pub. A veritable New Cross institution, you can visit Afrikan Boy in *'Lidl'* one night, then look for *'Elvis'* with These New Puritans on another. Picture CBGBs, but with more neon. Hop on a bus and 15 minutes later you'll be in **Peckham** with a collective of kids called **!WOWOW!** Led by the 'art-shaman' Matthew !WOWOW!, they do all sorts of fun stuff, like have week-long parties in squats and hold art events that include performance artists recreating the zombie dance steps from Michael Jackson's *Thriller*.

Amersham Arms

001

388 New Cross Road, SE14 6TY
020 8469 1499
www.amersham-arms.co.uk
Tube: New Cross
Open: Mon-Wed 12:00-00:00, Thu-Sat 12:00-03:00, Sun 12:00-00:00

Managed by the savvy bunch responsible for Camden's
Lock Tavern and the brilliant 'Adventures In The Beetroot
Field' nights, the Amersham Arms is the best pub south of
the river. With listings any club would kill for, a menu that
falls the right side of 'gastro', and a relaxed, friendly atmosphere, this hybrid pub epitomises what we Londoners have
come to expect from our local drinking-holes. Upstairs,
you'll find the Take Courage Gallery, a curated space showing works from established and new artists. But it's the 300-
capacity music space out back that makes the Amersham so
amazing. The talented team at the helm ensures a constant
stream of the best bands and top DJs every night of the week
— it's staggering. We wholeheartedly recommend you get
yourselves down here as soon as possible.

01,02,03 Amersham Arms; photography by Billa

Carling Academy Brixton

002

211 Stockwell Road, SW9 9SL
020 7771 3000
www.brixton-academy.co.uk
Tube: Brixton
Open: Performance times vary

The multi-award winning Brixton Academy (as it is better
known) presents some of the capital's best live music
shows. Its 5,000 capacity (and the largest fixed stage in
Europe) guarantees gigs by world-famous acts. But it's not
just the attraction of ticket sales for these artists. The
theatre's Grade II-listed status and art deco interior prevent
it from becoming another soulless concert venue; instead
the Academy povides an atmospheric setting in which to
play to fans. This alone was enough of a pull for Madonna
who performed a gig here in 2000. Stars who have
preceded or succeeded her on this stage include the Beastie
Boys, The Strokes, Bob Dylan, Prince, The Clash and the
late James Brown. The B-Boy Championships and DMC
World DJ Championships also take place here every year.

The Deptford Arms

003

52 Deptford High Street, SE8 4RT. T: 020 8692 1180
W: www.myspace.com/deptfordarms Tube: New Cross
Open: Mon-Sat 11:00-01:00, Sun 11:00-00:00

'Free jukebox, free arcade games and £2 pints every day between 5 and 8.' Need we say more? Well, yes actually, because this is just the tip of the iceberg. The Deptford Arms
is owned by the same people as the New Cross Inn, so you
know you're in good hands here. Indulging their cultured
side, there's a cool little art gallery downstairs but don't worry, it's not tamed anything upstairs. Here, you'll find the same
debauched mayhem we've come to expect from a good South
East pub of late. The Catapult Club, a weekly event expos-
ing up-and-coming bands, comes highly recommended, as
does the weekly quiz, where you can use brain cells while
simultaneously destroying them with cheap alcohol.

05 The Coronet; photography by Billa

04 The Coronet; photography by Grace Pattison

The Montague Arms   004

289 Queens Road, SE15 2PA
020 7639 4923
www.myspace.com/themontaguearms
Tube: New Cross Gate
Open: Mon-Sat 19:30-00:00 (closed Wed), Sun 11:00-00:00

Festooned with taxidermic oddities (a zebra in the middle of the pub, anyone?), nautical paraphernalia and all manner of other weird ornaments, this place is just insane. Its lysergic decor, cheap drinks and great food (the Sunday roasts are legendary) have long made it a favourite with the local Goldsmiths students. With their quirky leftfield tastes, 'The Monty' is now a renowned live music venue too, regularly playing host to alternative acts you'd expect to find down the ICA, rather than a south London boozer. If you are Deep South, there is no excuse not to visit. And, as a glance at the listings will testify, you never know what to expect from this mad little boozer.

New Cross Inn   005

323 New Cross Road, SE14 6AS. T: 020 8692 1866
W: www.myspace.com/newcrossinn Tube: New Cross. Open: Mon-Sat 12:00-02:00, Sun 12:00-00:00

Dark, grubby and filled with students, aesthetically, the New Cross Inn might not be to everyone's taste. But bloody hell, do they know how to throw a party! A key player in the south's continued assault on the beachhead of Shoreditch cool, this pub-cum-club single-handedly put New Cross back on the map a few years ago, becoming the spiritual centre for the then 'New Cross scene', which birthed bands like Klaxons. Blessed with a big stage (by pub standards, anyway) the New Cross Inn is a great live gig venue with sufficient space to let the kids go mental, while the rest drink their drinks without getting an elbow in the eye. Weekly events and line-ups read like a who's who of the latest and greatest, yet it all goes down without the folded-arm, po-faced posturing so common in other parts of London.

The Windmill   006

22 Blenheim Gardens, SW2 5BZ. T: 020 8671 0700
W: www.windmillbrixton.co.uk Tube: Brixton. Open: Times vary
Doors normally 20:00-late

The Windmill is one of the key pubs on London's live music scene. Its 100% focus on quality ensures a steady flow of burgeoning acts to its stage, many of whom have gone on to enjoy commercial success: Hot Chip, Jamie T, Klaxons, Maximo Park and Pop Levi. An authentically scruffy gig-venue, it offers cheap drinks and a dirty solace in which to hear the sounds rising from the underground.

The Coronet Theatre

26-28 New Kent Road, SE1 6TJ. T: 020 7701 1500
W: www.coronettheatre.co.uk Tube: Elephant and Castle. Open: Times vary

This venue is the site of numerous gigs and club nights. Oasis and Primal Scream through to CSS, M.I.A and The Horrors all played shows here, and it also hosts the ever popular Underage Club and secretsundaze parties. This place is licensed to sell alcohol until 7a.m. on the weekends, which will come as good news to party-goers.

Plan B

418 Brixton Road, SW9 7AY. T: 0870 1165 421. W: www.plan-brixton.co.uk
Tube: Brixton. Open: Mon-Wed 17:00-late, Thu 17:00-03:00, Fri 17:00-04:00
Sat 19:00-05:00, Sun 19:00-03:00

Nice bar/club venue with a dedicated team of promoters who introduce club nights ranging from hip hop and funk to soul, house and disco. Sir Norman Jay, Basement Jaxx, KRS-One, Aaron La Crate and Mark Ronson are just some of the acts that have appeared at Friday's weekly party, Fidgit. Thursday's b-boy battle, Throwdown is a night of breaking, popping and scratch battles, where the only attitude you experience is on the dance floor.

The Prince Albert

418 Coldharbour Lane, SW9 8LF. T: 020 7274 3771. Tube: Brixton
Open: Sun-Thu 12:00-23:00

The Prince Albert is Brixton's most popular boozer. Live bands (usually punk), music quizzes, poetry readings, DJs, Sunday roasts and a beer garden, have secured The Prince Albert the loyalty of locals and visitors, old and young alike. If you're in this neighbourhood and only have time for one drink, head here.

The Prince and Dex Club

467-469 Brixton Road, SW9 8HH. T: 020 7326 4455. W: www.dexclub.co.uk
Tube: Brixton. Open: The Prince: Mon-Tue 12:00-00:00, Wed-Thu 12:00-02:00
Fri-Sat 11:00-04:00, Sun 11:00-00:00. Dex: Open to members durning the week
and non-members at weekends

The Prince in Brixton offers DJs, a roof terrace and a games room. But this isn't just a pub, the site (est. 1800) also houses a members bar and an art deco boutique hotel on the first and second floors. The Dex is the first of its kind in this area, *offering eight stylish bedrooms and suites from £80 per night. Guests have free access to the rooftop bar, hot tubs and sun loungers, and there are rumours that turntables will be available in the rooms soon. The Dex is currently only open to non-members at weekends.*

ebony bones

Q: Where's your favourite place to go for a drink?
"There's that nice little diner on Curtain Road, I quite like — me and the girls often go there for a milkshake and a giggle."

Q: What areas do you feel represent London's richest fashion veins? "Anywhere with a good charity shop really. You can often find me in clothes from outside The Salvation Army, but I make a lot of what I wear and most of it costs less than a Happy Meal."

Ebony Bones; photography by Laurie Fletcher

SOUTH London's retail landscape is pretty barren, it must be said. The creative boutiques are often run on short-term leases or out of squats, and given their untenable nature, can appear and disappear within a matter of months. New Cross and Deptford are the most fashionable areas, and the retail landscape here should change dramatically over the next few years. But at the moment, great stores are thin on the ground in this part of London.

Borough Market

8 Southwark Street, SE1 1TL. T: 020 7926 9177
W: www.boroughmarket.org.uk Open: Thu 11:00-17:00
Fri 12:00-18:00, Sat 21:00-16:00

A gourmet and wholesale food market frequented by top chefs and food lovers. Award-winning produce is on sale, with many traders offering freshly prepared food which you can eat while you shop (the most popular is the chorizo & rocket sandwich stall — expect queues). Foods range from fresh and cured meats, cakes, olive oil and chutneys to freshly baked breads and seafood. Don't miss the Neal's Yard Creamery, which is situated just outside the market.

Brixton Market

Electric Avenue, Granville Arcade, Station Arcade and Market Row. Tube: Brixton. Open: Mon-Sat 10:00-18:00, Wed 10:00-13:00

Brixton Market is the largest Caribbean market in Europe, stretching across several areas including Electric Avenue, Granville Arcade, Station Arcade and Market Row. Vintage and retro clothes, vinyl & CDs, electric goods, exotic food and bric-a brac are the wares on offer

at this vibrant street market, and there are plenty of snacking opportunities courtesy of the West Indian food stalls. Look out for the Brixton Arts and Crafts market on Tunstall Road.

Deptford Market

Douglas Way & Deptford High Street, SE8
BR/DLR: Deptford. Open: Wed, Fri & Sat 21:00-17:00

This market is a hunting ground for the local Deptford/New Cross fashionistas. Aside from the usual market tat, you'll find clothes, furniture, books, magazines and vinyl.

Greenwich Market

Greenwich Church Street. W: www.greenwichmarket.net DLR: Greenwich. Open: Thu-Sun 09:30-17:30

Greenwich Market specialises in arts and crafts, selling records, antiques, books, clothing and so much more. Vintage outlet, The Observatory is an essential visit. Upstairs offers a good variety of apparel for men and women along with footwear and accessories. The stock is reasonably priced and you should pick up something great as Londoners don't really descend on this market that often.

HQ London

88 Brixton Village, Coldharbour Lane, SW9 8PS
T: 020 7274 4664. W: www.hqlondon.co.uk
Tube: Brixton. Open: Mon-Sat 12:00-18:30
(Wed 12:00-16:30)

A specialist hip hop store selling graffiti product, vinyl, CDs and DVDs, books and magazines. HQ offers one of the largest selections of aerosol paint in the UK by the leading brands including Montana and Molotow.

Prangsta Costumiers

304 New Cross Road, SE14 6AF. T: 020 8694 9869
W: www.prangsta.co.uk Open: Mon-Sat 11:00-19:00

Prangsta Costumiers showcases some of the nicest bespoke fashion in the capital. Melanie Wilson's two-floor space is worthy of a bit part in a Jim Henson movie, with sewing machines whirring furiously in the corner, and every inch of space immersed in lace, silk and intricate embroidery. The room offers fancy dress, second-hand vintage and Melanie's own Prangsta label, and it also acts as a mentoring haven for undergraduate fashion students.

Radio Days

87 Lower Marsh, SE1 7AB. T: 020 7928 0800
W: www.radiodaysvintage.co.uk Tube: Waterloo
Open: Mon-Sat 10:00-18:00 (Fri 10:00-19:00)

This quirky vintage boutique sells fashion and memorabilia from the 1920s-1970s. Whether you're a collector or a retro fiend, you'll find all manner of goodies here from clothing, magazines, homeware and accessories to telephones, radios and sheet music. If you like this place, try the nearby '60s and '70s retro boutique, What the Butler Wore, at no.131.

TRAID Brixton

2 Acre Lane, SW2 5SG. T: 020 7326 4330
W: www.traid.org.uk Tube: Brixton. Open: Mon–Sat 10:00-18:00, Sun 11:00-17:00

TRAID takes unwanted clothes intended for the landfill and reworks them into contemporary pieces.

New Cross Gallery

3 Lewisham Way, SE14 6PP. T: 020 8469 1415. W: www.newcrossgallery.com Tube: New Cross or New Cross Gate. Open: Tue-Sat 11:00-17:30

Pooling the artistry of south London's creative epicentre, the New Cross Gallery dedicates itself to urban art and photography. Founded by Thomas Chan, the art and installation space sits in the heart of New Cross (opposite Goldsmiths) with new exhibitions showing on a near-monthly basis, most recently, the UK artist, Mudwig. Highly recommended.

listed galleries

The Arthouse Gallery

140 Lewisham Way, SE14 6PD. T: 020 8694 9011 Tube: New Cross Gate. Open: Wed-Sun 12:00-18:00

The Arthouse Gallery exhibits works by graduates of Goldsmiths college. If you've got an eye for talent-spotting, this is a good place to view and invest in newcomers.

Take Courage Gallery

(Upstairs at Amersham Arms), 388 New Cross Road, SE14 6TY. T: 020 8469 1499 W: www.amersham-arms.co.uk Tube: New Cross Open: Sun-Wed 12:00-00:00, Thu-Sat 12:00-late

A curated space upstairs at the Amersham Arms pub, which shows works by local artists.

New Cross Gallery featuring the work of Mudwig. Photography courtesy of the New Cross Gallery. Artwork © Mudwig, 2008.

Photography by Ed Whatling

SICKBOY ^{ARTIST}

Q: Where's the best place to eat out? "The best place to eat is **Tesco**, because it's cheap so I can save money to buy more beer."

Q: Where do you go out in London? "Working and living in east London, it's nice to get out of the area to do different things. A good alternative is the **Bloomsbury Bowling Lanes**: you can bowl, it's got karaoke booths and there are music gigs. The best music nights are **Lowlife** [Corsica Studios in Elephant & Castle] or **David Mancuso** [legendary DJ from The Loft in NYC] at **The Light Bar**."

N E W   Y O U N G   P O N Y   C L U B

PHOTOGRAPHY BY DEAN CHALKLEY

Q: SOMEONE ARRIVES IN LONDON FOR ONLY 4 HOURS AND YOU ARE THEIR GUIDE. WHERE DO YOU TAKE THEM? "PROBABLY WESTMINSTER AS YOU COULD HAVE AN HOUR WANDERING AROUND THE SIGHTS, THEN A QUICK GO ON THE WHEEL, RACE AROUND TATE MODERN AND THEN INTO SOHO FOR FOOD AND RECORD BUYING. OR AS AN ALTERNATIVE, MAYBE UP TO THE NAGS HEAD AND FINSBURY PARK, THEN DOWN TO DALSTON AND THE MARKETS AROUND NORTH EAST LONDON JUST SO THEY COULD GET A FLAVOUR OF WHAT LONDON'S REALLY LIKE… AND EAT DECENT TRINIDADIAN FOOD." Q: BEST PLACES TO BUY MUSIC? "PHONICA, SOUNDS OF THE UNIVERSE, PURE GROOVE (AND THE NOW SADLY GONE ROUGH TRADE CENTRAL IN COVENT GARDEN). I WOULD DEFINITELY TAKE A NEWCOMER TO LONDON TO PURE GROOVE AS IT IS REALLY OUT OF THE WAY AND WE COULD TAKE IN THE SIGHTS OF GLORIOUS CAMDEN ON THE JOURNEY." Q: WHERE'S YOUR FAVOURITE PLACE TO EAT OUT IN LONDON? "ANY OF THOSE VIETNAMESE RESTAURANTS ON KINGSLAND ROAD. THEY ARE ALL BRILL."

West

'West-lizzy is da-bomb'. Oh, really? Maybe to confused chavs who twist their fingers up in 'W' signs and think **Tupac** is still alive, but to the rest of us, west London is best known for the street party that attracts like **2 million people** and gives PC Plod a chance to cop a feel from overzealous party-goers. The **Notting Hill Carnival** is like splashing your face in a bucket full of bass and spicy jerk-chicken. With the added possibility of getting your ass kicked by a **gang of kids** in hoodies and New Era hats. Which is probably why those affluent types that reside in Kensington, Chelsea and Fulham stay in their mansions and watch the highlights of the carnival on the evening news. West London has **money to burn.** It's so close to central London, that the pound signs have trickled down to its many districts and its residents use wads of money to fan themselves in the summer. Luckily, their servants can still head down to **Portobello Road** market to pick up a bargain. You may even find that huge dollar-sign chain and vintage Cazal glasses you were looking for. Which would be the perfect attire to rock to Notting Hill's **yOyO.** It's where all the '80s babies congregate and share the dance floor with **Kanye West** and Mark Ronson. Which makes us wonder why they never showed us any of this stuff in the *Notting Hill* movie?

Traditionally, the districts immediately west of central London are the province of the filthy rich. Streets lined with immaculately-manicured townhouses, designer boutiques and expensive eateries punctuate this part of town. Yet, for all its upmarket glamour, there's a distinct lack of diversity when it comes to retail and nightlife, especially for your average Joe (that's you), looking for a good time. Go to Harrods and Harvey Nichols, see Portobello Road Market; this part of town is by no means bereft of interesting stuff, just, there's a sparser distribution here than elsewhere. Ultimately, the dynamic of this area is set by its affluent inhabitants: stylish but safe.

12 ACKLAM ROAD   001

12 Acklam Road, W10 5QZ
020 8960 9331
www.12acklamroadclub.com
Tube: Ladbroke Grove
Open: Mon-Sun 21:00-late

Formerly known as Neighbourhood, this venue rebranded itself late-2007, and is now one of the area's most popular live music and DJ clubs. Situated just off Portobello Road, the two-floor space has started to pull in some of London's finest promoters and acts, with Nightmoves (Kitsuné), Joakim (Tigersushi) and Zombie Disco Squad playing here recently. A large party space with a great sound system, 12 Acklam Road is drawing clubbers back to Notting Hill.

Bush Hall   002

310 Uxbridge Road, W12 7LJ
020 8222 6955
www.bushhallmusic.co.uk
Tube: Shepherds Bush Central
Open: Performance times vary

An historic live music venue, Bush Hall is home to legendary acts, major pop stars, and up-and-coming artists. Built in 1905 as a ballroom dance hall, it later became a bingo hall which was used as a rehearsal space for The Who. Bush Hall has since carved a reputation as a top music theatre attracting Kings Of Leon, Lily Allen, Nick Cave & The Bad Seeds and Jamie T recently.

Mau Mau   003

265 Portobello Road, W11 1LR
020 7229 8528
www.maumaubar.com
Tube: Ladbroke Grove
Open: Mon-Thu 12:00-23:30, Fri-Sat 12:00-02:3

This ultra-chilled bar is, in our opinion, the best in the west for watching the world go by. Located in the middle of a bustling market street, and serving the best coffee and cocktails on Portobello Road, it's an ideal place to meet friends after shopping at Saturday's market.

Notting Hill Arts Club   004

21 Notting Hill Gate, W11 3JQ
020 7598 5226
www.nottinghillartsclub.com
Tube: Notting Hill Gate
Open: Times vary (yOyO: Every Thursday, 19:00-02:00. Death Disco: Every Wednesday, 18:00-02:00)

Home to club-kid party, yOyO, the Notting Hill Arts Club is the leading nightspot in this neighbourhood for live music, parties, and art and culture showcases. The clientele varies according to the night you visit. Seb Chew & Leo Greenslade's Thursday hip hop and soul party, yOyO is a night for London's most fashionable. Alan McGee's weekly Wednesday club, Death Disco attracts indie fans with its quality unsigned talent plus guest DJs like Jah Wobble and Courtney Love. Most nights, you'll find a mixed, friendly crowd soaking up the intimate atmosphere. This club has a huge appreciation for all genres so the music policy swings wildly from one night to the next. The arts programme is no less diverse, with graffiti and contemporary artists exhibiting regularly. The common thread connecting the music and art, is quality, and it's the reason why the Notting Hill Arts Club is as popular today as it was a decade ago.

Notting Hill Carnival

Notting Hill   005
020 7727 0072
www.nottinghillcarnival.biz
Tube: Notting Hill Gate
Open: August Bank Holiday (last weekend of the month)

Now attracting an estimated 2 million visitors a year, Notting Hill Carnival is Europe's biggest street party, second in the world to carnival capital, Rio. For two days every August Bank Holiday, Old London Town erupts in an explosion of colour, costume, cuisine and music. From humble beginnings as a small celebration among Notting Hill's West Indian community, in its near fifty years, the scope and scale has widened to incorporate African, South American and Caribbean influences, symbolising London's multi-cultural diversity. Music is as varied as the party-goers in attendance. The steel pan bands accompanying the parades provide the basic sonic motif, but from here everything scatterguns. Quaking speaker stacks distort the air with bowel-slackening bass, as sound systems play-out the Dub, Reggae and Soca synonymous with festivities. Turn a corner, however, and you find something different: Hip Hop, Drum 'n' Bass, Funk, Afro-Beat — dance music in all its guises. The best party, of course, comes courtesy of Sir Norman Jay and his legendary Good Times stage. London's most beloved DJ and man-of-the-people, bottlenecks all the weekend's musical styles, distilling, what for many, is the Carnival's true soundtrack. Make sure you get yourself here.

Notting Hill Carnival photography by Che Blomfield, see page 138

Shepherd's Bush Empire

Shepherd's Bush Green, W12 8TT. T: 020 8354 3300. W: www.shepherds-bush-empire.co.uk Tube: Shepherd's Bush. Open: Performance times vary

An award-winning live music venue housed in a grand theatre on Shepherd's Bush Green. The artists who perform at this venue range from pop acts to rock gods of the past and present. Countless legends have graced this stage over its 100-year history, including the Sex Pistols, Johnny Cash, Iggy Pop and the Rolling Stones.

Trailer Happiness

177 Portobello Road, W11 2DY. T: 020 7727 2700. W: www.trailerh.com Tube: Ladbroke Grove. Open: Tue-Sun 17:00-00:00

This Notting Hill tiki bar is an intimate bar and kitchen with DJs most nights. If you're after an early evening cocktail, head here.

Under the Westway

Westbourne Studios, 242 Acklam Road, W10 5JJ. T: 020 7575 3123. W: www.westbournestudios.com Tube: Westbourne Park. Open: Mon-Fri from 08:30, Fri 08:30-02:00, Sat 18:00-02:00

A workspace meets creative hangout, frequented by the Studios' media and design workers. Its gallery, exhibition space and auditorium are often used for events like the Portobello Film Festival, along with a varied programme of art exhibitions. On-site bar and restaurant, Under the Westway is a popular choice for the local residents, boasting a pool table, 100-seat cinema plus live music and DJs during the week.

The Westbourne

101 Westbourne Park Villas, W2 5ED. T: 020 7221 1332. W: www.thewestbourne.com Tube: Royal Oak. Open: Mon-Sat 11:00-23:00, Sun 12:00-23:00

The Westbourne is a warm and inviting gastro pub in the upmarket Westbourne Park Villas. Attracting celebrities and Notting Hill twenty-somethings, The Westbourne is best on Sunday afternoons when the staff anticipate hangovers and prepare Bloody Marys, lining them on the bar for when you arrive. Whether relaxing on the heated outside terrace, or in the cosy pub itself, this is a great boozer and a good place to grab a bite to eat. The pub's busy all year round, but particularly so in summer, when the crowds spill onto the street.

Notting Hill Carnival; photography by Che Blomfield

The Dispensary   006

200 Kensington Park Road, W11 1VR
020 7727 8797
www.thedispensary.net
Tube: Notting Hill Gate
Open: Mon-Sat 10:30-18:30, Thu 10:30-19:30, Sun 12:00-17:00

Arriving in Notting Hill in 1994, The Dispensary instantly struck a chord by offering edgier clothing labels to the local fashion obsessives. Its immediate success saw the boutique branch out with a second womenswear outlet in Soho. The Notting Hill branch is still one of the more fashion-focused retailers in the area, selling an edited selection of women's and menswear, accessories and footwear by Servanne Gaxotte, Orla Kiely, Maria Bonita, Bi La Li, Oliver Spencer and Without Prejudice.

THE DISPENSARY in Soho is at 9 Newburgh Street, W1 7RB
T: 020 7287 8145. Tube: Oxford Circus

THE GARBSTORE   007

188 Kensington Park Road, W11 2ES
www.garbstore.com
Tube: Ladbroke Grove
Open: Mon-Sat 10:00-17:30

The Garbstore is a new streetwear label and boutique for men, recently launched in Notting Hill by Ian Paley, the founder and designer of One True Saxon. Paying homage to the greatest subcultural fashions, plus menswear from the post-war period, this label takes classic vintage styles as its blueprint, and marries it with contemporary design. The result is a really nice selection of product that has been authentically created on vintage machines.

Jeff (founder of One of a Kind); photography by Naughty James. See page 140

Honest Jon's   008

278 Portobello Road, W10 5TE
020 8969 9822
www.honestjons.com
Tube: Ladbroke Grove
Open: Mon-Sat 10:00-18:00, Sun 11:00-17:00

A purveyor of fine music for over 25 years, Honest Jon's is a west London institution. Perched at the Ladbroke Grove end of Portobello Road, the record store champions London's diverse music scene with unparalleled knowledge and passion. Frequented by DJs and collectors, the store has a specialist jazz and world music section in the vaults, while upstairs you can dig up everything from reggae 7"s to house, hip hop, funk or broken beat. 2002 saw the launch of the Honest Jon's record label (co-owned by Damon Albarn), which reflects the shop's world music policy.

ONE OF A KIND 009

259 Portobello Road, W11 1LR
020 7792 5284
www.1kind.com
Tube: Ladbroke Grove
Open: Mon-Sun 11:00-18:00, Sat 10:30-18:00

An excellent little vintage shop for women, packed from floor to ceiling with clothes, bags and accessories. A bit like your stylish grandmother's closet, you'll find flapper dresses (original from the era), designer evening gowns, and handbags in every size and style imaginable. There's also a walk-in boxroom crammed with shoes and boots. Remember the vintage dress that Sadie Frost wore to The Oscars? She bought it here — the supermodels and celebrities have been shopping here ever since. The product doesn't come cheap (shoes cost approx £140) which might explain why the shop is so full of stock. But this place deals only in the highest quality vintage pieces and is great for those looking to invest in a one-off treasured item. Further along the road (No. 253), you'll find sister store, One of a Kind Too.

PORTOBELLO MARKET

Portobello Road (Westbourne Grove, Elgin Crescent), W11
www.portobelloroad.co.uk
Tube: Notting Hill Gate or Ladbroke Grove
Open: Sat approx 06:30-17:30

The legendary Portobello Market is where you'll find some of the finest vintage clothing in London. Every Saturday, along a two mile stretch, market traders sell antiques, jewellery, art, food and homewares alongside the more traditional market bric-a-brac and knock-off designer goods. The Westway area is dedicated to the fashion market, featuring small, independent designers, antique fashions, fabric and accessories alongside second-hand clothing dealers. There are fashion stalls throughout the Portobello Road area, selling costume design and jewellery, and if you head to Goldbourne Road, you'll find more retro garbs. Portobello Market is the world's biggest antiques market so expect it to be crowded on Saturdays. If you get lost, head over to the information booth at the junction of Portobello Road and Westbourne Grove.

010

PREEN 011

5 Portobello Green Arcade, Acklam Workspace, Acklam Road, W10 5QZ
020 8968 1542
Tube: Ladbroke Grove
Open: Thu-Sat 11:00-18:00

British fashion label, Preen, is a regular at London Fashion Week, and their collections are stocked in top boutiques throughout the capital. This studio and shop is the label's home.

Rellik photography by Naughty James

RELLIK 012

8 Golborne Road, W10 5NW
020 8962 0089
ww.relliklondon.co.uk
Tube: Westbourne Grove
Open: Tue-Sat 10:00-18:00

Rellik is held in high regard by dedicated vintage hunters, and while it's pricier than many, it's better than most. A favourite of London fashionistas, its superb and unrivalled collection of on-trend designer one-offs, vintage couture and rare retro gear causes much salivating from locals and visiting Hollywood actresses alike. Vivienne Westwood pieces from the Sex boutique era, early Comme des Garçons, Punk, Ossie Clark and Pucci; it's all here.

ROUGH TRADE WEST   013

130 Talbot Road, W11 1JA
020 7229 8541
Tube: Ladbroke Grove
www.roughtrade.com
Open: Mon-Sat 10:00-18:30, Sun 12:00-17:00

In 1976, Rough Trade opened its doors in Notting Hill and started a revolution. Relentless pioneers of quality music, the label has lent a helping hand to countless great bands over the years. This shop mirrors Rough Trade's wide and obsessive interest with underground music, and stocks an excellent selection of vinyl and CDs. Individual tastes are catered for, so whether it's hip hop, jazz fusion or folk, feel safe in the hands of the knowledgeable Rough Trade.
ROUGH TRADE EAST: Dray Walk (off Brick Lane), E1 6QL. T: 020 7392 7788
Tube: Liverpool Street

Supra   014

249 Portobello Road, W11 1LT
020 7243 3130
www.suprafly.com
Tube: Ladbroke Grove
Open: Mon-Thu 11:00-18:00, Fri-Sat 10:00-18:00, Sun 12:00-17:00

Recently reunited, the Supra men's and women's boutiques are now in one store, halfway down Portobello Road. Specialising in designer streetwear, there's product here by Adidas, Penfield, Nike and Stüssy, plus accessories by London label, Tatty Devine.

World's End   015

430 King's Road, SW10 0LJ
020 7352 6551
www.viviennewestwood.co.uk
Tube: Sloane Square
Open: Mon-Sat 10:00-18:00

This is where it all began for Vivienne Westwood back in the 1970s. When punk exploded onto the streets of London, Westwood was running this boutique (then called Sex), alongside Malcolm McLaren. It was here that she designed her legendary punk fashions, and it was also where she kitted out the Sex Pistols with her outlandish designs. The original King's Road boutique is now a landmark; not only for Dame Viv's dedication to British fashion, but for the beautifully-designed shop front with its thirteen-hour clock face showing hands turning backwards — an acknowledgement of the past in her creations and a nod to the Westwood defiance that we've come to expect. World's End reflects the era that pushed the designer to the forefront of fashion. It is thus an outlet for her more experimental designs plus plenty of the original styles that secured her status as a global fashion icon.

295

295 Portobello Road, W11 1LB. T: 020 8964 5603
Tube: Ladbroke Grove. Open: Tue-Sat 10:30-17:30

One for the boys. Selling period clothing and accessories, this shop is more about cheap vintage threads than must-have labels but that's not to say that you won't stumble across a designer piece. There's a small section for women too.

aimé

32 Ledbury Road, W11 2AB. T: 020 7221 7070
W: www.aimelondon.com Tube: Notting Hill Gate
Open: Mon-Sat 10:00-18:30

A Parisian-focused boutique in Notting Hill exclusively flaunting French product, including rare fashion labels, homeware, music, accessories and books.

Appleby Vintage

95 Westbourne Park Villas, W2 5ED. T: 020 7229
7772. W: www.applebyvintage.com
Tube: Royal Oak. Open: Fri-Sat afternoon. During
the week, phone ahead to make an appointment

An upmarket vintage boutique run by Jane Appleby selling a superbly-edited range of clothing, footwear and accessories.

Austique

330 King's Road, SW3 5UR. T: 020 7376 4555
W: www.austique.co.uk Tube: Sloane Square
Open: Mon-Sat 10:30-19:00, Sun 12:00-17:00

Austique is a King's Road-based emporium of femininity dedicated to hard-to-find labels. The buyers hunt down designers and denim brands that are making waves internationally (Karen Walker, Thurley, Cohen et Sabine), and showcase their wares alongside bath & beauty products, lingerie, swimwear and gifts.

Dolly Diamond

51 Pembridge Road, W11 3HG. T: 020 7792 2479
W: www.dollydiamond.com Tube: Notting Hill Gate. Open: Mon-Fri 10:30-18:30, Sat 09:30-18:30 Sun 12:00-18:00

Dolly Diamond sells assorted retro goods from swimsuits and spectacles, to retro ball gowns and dinner suits. A specialist in evening wear for men and women, stock covers the 1920s-1970s, with a price tag to suit all budgets.

Feathers

176 Westbourne Grove, W11 2RW. T: 020 7243 8800
W: www.feathersfashion.com Tube: Notting Hill Gate. Open: Mon-Sat 10:00-18:00, Sun 12:00-18:00

This designer store in Notting Hill features high-end fashion labels like Alexander McQueen. The Knightsbridge branch is one of the few outlets in the capital to stock the acclaimed British label, Basso & Brooke.

Feathers photography by Naughty James

FEATHERS Knightsbridge: 42 Hans Crescent, SW1X 0LZ
T: 020 7589 5802. Tube: Knightsbridge

Harrods

87-135 Brompton Road, SW1X 7XL. W: www.harrods.com Tube: Knightsbridge or Sloane Square Open: Mon-Sat 10:00-20:00, Sun 12:00-18:00

This world-famous department store needs no introduction. Worth a visit for the food hall alone, you'll find all the top designer labels from around the globe here.

Harvey Nichols

109-125 Knightsbridge, SW1X 7RJ. T: 020 7235 5000
W: www.harveynichols.com Tube: Knightsbridge
Open: Mon-Fri 10:00-20:00, Sat 10:00-20:00, Sun 12:00-18:00

A luxury department store in Knightsbridge stocking major designers and smaller independent labels. This is the Harvey Nichols flagship store so expect their very best stock.

Intoxica Records

231 Portobello Road, W11 1LT. T: 020 7229 8010
Tube: Ladbroke Grove. Open: Mon-Fri 22:30-18:30 Sat 10:00-18:30

Intoxica deals in new and rare vinyl, with a special focus on the 1960s and 1970s. The tiki-inspired record store is full of collectable vinyl spanning '60s beat, jazz, soul, punk, ska, reggae and '50s R'n'B, plus the latest independent releases.

Matches

Matches Mens is at 60-64 Ledbury Road, W11 2AJ T: 020 72210255. Matches Womens is at 22-24 Ledbury Road, W11 2AG. T: 020 7221 0255 W: www.matchesfashion.com Tube: Notting Hill Gate Open: Mon-Sat 10:00-18:00, Sun 11:00-17:00

Matches has the largest selection of designer clothing in this neighbourhood. Product is sourced straight from the catwalk and includes the latest collections by Stella McCartney, Alexander McQueen, Hussein Chalayan and Chloé, as well as Nudie and Acne.

One

30 Ledbury Road, W11 2AB. T: 020 7221 5330
W: www.only0ne.com Tube: Notting Hill Gate

As the name suggests, this store exclusively stocks one-off garments for women. While the stock can err on the 'safe' side of style, a good hunt should turn up a gem.

Pistol Panties

75 Westbourne Park Road, W2 5QH. T: 020 7229 5286. W: www.pistolpanties.com Tube: Royal Oak Open: Mon-Sat 11:00-18:00

Whichever style of swimwear you go for (pin-up, disco, femme fatale), Pistol Panties will have you looking like a Bond Girl with its incredible selection of bikinis and bathing suits, which are weapons in their own right. For the best beachwear in town, nobody does it better.

Question Air

229 Westbourne Grove, W11 2SE. T: 020 7221 8163 W: www.question-air.com Tube: Ladbroke Grove Open: Mon-Wed 10:30-18:00, Thu-Sat 10:00-18:30 Sun 12:00-17:30

Question Air sells a wide selection of labels for men and women including Vivienne Westwood, Nobody, Antipodium, APRIL77, Betsey Johnson and Paul Smith. The store also boasts an extensive denim collection.

Retro Man / Retro Woman

20 & 32 Pembridge Road, W11 3HN. T: 020 7221 2055. W: www.mveshops.co.uk Tube: Notting Hill Gate. Open: Daily 10:00-20:00

A second-hand shop selling designer threads, shoes and accessories at knock-down prices. The 30-year-old Retro Woman at no.20, retails jewellery, clothing and accessories from the biggest labels out there. Shoes come courtesy of sought-after designers including: Manalo Bhlanik (£60), Gucci (£30) and Miu Miu (£50). There's also a good selection of purses and handbags from the likes of Vivienne Westwood (£40) and Sergio Rossi (£30). The basement is a haven for rummagers, with rail upon rail of clothing, belts and hats. Retro Man is at no.32 Pembridge Road.

Sharpeye

Unit 26 Portobello Green, W10 5TZ. T: 020 7896 9333. W: sharpeye-31-01-60.com Tube: Ladbroke Grove. Open: Mon-Thu 11:00-18:00, Fri-Sat 10:00-18:00, Sun 12:00-17:00

This streetwear store for men and women was recently introduced by Barrie Sharpe, the designer/musician once behind the Duffer of St George label. His new Sharpeye label and boutique in Notting Hill sells the full collection including custom-designed lowrider bikes.

Size?

200 Portobello Road, W11 1LB. T: 020 7792 8494 W: www. size-online.co.uk Tube: Ladbroke Grove Open: Mon-Thu 11:00-18:00, Fri-Sat 10:00-18:00 Sun 11:00-17:00

Sneaker store, Size? stocks the latest steppers around with plenty of its own exclusives. For full review, see page 89.

TRAID Remade

61 Westbourne Grove, W2 4UA. T: 020 7221 2421 W: www.traid.org.uk Tube: Queensway. Open: Mon-Sat 10:00-18:00, Sun 11:00-17:00

TRAID is a chain of charity shops that takes clothes intended for the landfill, and has its team of young designers re-work them into contemporary pieces. They also sell vintage clothing.

Urban Outfitters

36-38 Kensington High Street, W8 4PF. T: 020 7761 1001. W: www.urbanoutfitters.co.uk Tube: High Street Kensington. Open: Mon-Sat 10:00-19:00 (Thu 10:00-20:00), Sun 12:00-18:00

American retail emporium selling independent labels and vintage clothing, plus books, vinyl, footwear and accessories for men and women.

PHOTOGRAPHY

01 Appleby photography by Naughty James

02 One photography by Naughty James

03 One photography by Naughty James

Allsopp Contemporary 016

Address: 8 Conlan Street, W10 5AR. T: 020 8960 5355. W: www.allsoppcontemporary.com Tube: Ladbroke Grove. Open: Mon-Fri 10:00-18:00, Sat 12:00-18:00

This art space in Notting Hill has presented some great shows over the last few years, including *Natural Selection: British Graffiti* which featured acclaimed UK artists: Xenz, Insa, Conor Harrington and Wish One. The Allsopp Contemporary focuses on urban and contemporary art, with solo and group shows by home and internationally-grown artists. The sheer scale of the gallery space makes it ideal for a graffiti artist like Insa, who uses cars and bikes as his canvas in addition to wall-mounted works. This gallery is good at identifying talent and often secures shows with artists during their early careers. It's therefore a good spot for investing in rising artists from around the globe.

Electric Cinema 017

191 Portobello Road, W11 2ED
Box Office: 020 7908 9696
www.electriccinema.co.uk
Tube: Ladbroke Grove
Open: Times vary (call box office for details)

This is our favourite cinema in London for both art house and block-buster screenings. The spacious theatre is luxuriously appointed with leather seating, foot stools and tables for food and drink plus two-seater sofas. There's even a licensed bar at the rear serving champagne, beer and wine. In addition to main features, the Electric shows independent film, double bills (past and present) as well as classic cinema and festival film. There's only one screen, which means a limited number of viewings per day, however, it just requires a little organisation and the pre-booking of tickets (no less than one hour before a performance). This isn't the kind of cinema that serves a bucket of popcorn. Instead, you'll find a chef's selection of savoury hot snacks, chocolate brownies and locally-produced ice cream. All in all, the Electric is a superb cinema, where the film comes as a bonus.

EXHIBITION: *Natural Selection: British Graffiti*, 2005
Photography by Insa

ARTWORK: (Clockwise from centre): Insa, Xenz, Conor Harrington, Wish One. Read interviews with these artists at www.pimpguides.com

018 *The* **Saatchi Gallery**

Duke of York's HQ, King's Road, SW3 4RY
www.saatchi-gallery.co.uk
Tube: Sloane Square
Open: Times vary

The Saatchi Gallery is an important platform for UK contemporary artists. Over the last twenty years, it has exhibited the works of Damien Hirst, Andy Warhol and Jake & Dinos Chapman, and it's often the first to preview artists who have yet to break into the British market. Its new location in a 70,000 sq ft building on the King's Road, makes The Saatchi Gallery one of the largest contemporary art spaces in the world.

019 **Serpentine Gallery**

Kensington Gardens, W2 3XA
020 7402 6075
www.serpentinegallery.org
Tube: Knightsbridge, Lancaster Gate or South Kensington
Open: Daily 10:00–18:00

Set in the beautiful Kensington Gardens, the Serpentine Gallery is one of the most visited galleries in the capital. Exhibiting the works of the biggest and best modern and contemporary artists, it is a tranquil place to view paintings by artists like Gilbert & George and Damien Hirst. The latter curated an exhibition here featuring a private collection of works by his contemporaries: Tracey Emin, Francis Bacon, Banksy and Jeff Koons. Even Madonna has sponsored an exhibition at Serpentine, featuring the late, great NYC artist, Jean-Michel Basquiat. Offering film programmes, book launches and talks, plus artists working in a wide range of media, you'll find something here to suit every taste. The bookshop is also recommended.

KOENIG BOOKS AT THE SERPENTINE GALLERY
Open: Daily 10:00–18:00. T: 020 7706 4907

V&A

Cromwell Road, SW7 2RL
020 7942 2000
www.vam.ac.uk
Tube: South Kensington
Open: Daily 10.00-17.45 (Fri 10:00-22:00)

An art and design museum par excellence, that hosts world-beating cultural attractions covering fashion, photography, art, design and sculpture, as well as 3000 years worth of historical artefacts. The V&A attracts diverse exhibitors, small and major, including Vivienne Westwood, who also housed a retrospective catwalk show here. There's always something brilliant showing in one of the galleries, making it a regular destination for high and lowbrow culture aficionados, as well as students on research missions.

VIVIENNE WESTWOOD EXHIBITION; photography by Matthew Prall

020

Riverside Studios

Crisp Road, W6 9RL. T: 020 8237 1111. W: www.riversidestudios.co.uk Tube: Hammersmith. Open: Mon-Fri 08:30-23.00, Sat 12.00-23.00, Sun 12.00-22.30

Riverside Studios has hosted some of the most important performing arts, comedy, dance and music performances in recent history. Exhibitions by Yoko Ono and David Hockney have featured here, and the site has witnessed musical performances by the Rolling Stones and The Beatles. Contemporary international film, theatre and television run alongside one another in the studios, gallery and cinema, and there's often an experimental theatre production showing here. One theatre troupe faked an orgy on stage, its lead character performing a blow job on a 'volunteer' (an actor planted in the audience) who was sporting a prosthetic phallus — all in the name of creativity. The cinema focuses on international classics plus some rarely screened modern film. There's also a fully-licensed cafe/bar with a terrace and 'secret' garden.

The Andipa Gallery

162 Walton Street, SW3 2JL. T: 020 7589 2371. W: www.andipamodern.com Tube: South Kensington Open: Mon-Fri 09:30-18:00, Sat 11:00-18:00

A highbrow fine art gallery dealing in contemporary and modern artists such as Picasso and Warhol. The gallery recently exhibited its private collection of works by Banksy, and regularly has shows by new artists.

Hayward Gallery

Southbank Centre, Belvedere Road, SE1 8XX. T: 0871 663 2501. W: www.haywardgallery.org.uk Tube: Waterloo. Open: Daily 10:00-18:00 (Friday until 22:00)

Housed in the Southbank Centre, The Hayward Gallery offers a culturally rich programme of contemporary art, literature, music and performance art. The Hayward also invites speakers like Jake Chapman along to its Talks & Debates programme.

Michael Hoppen Gallery

3 Jubilee Place, SW3 3TD. T: 020 7352 3649. W: www.michaelhoppengallery.com Tube: South Kensington or Sloane Square. Open: Tue-Fri 12:00-18:00, Sat 10:30-16:00

This acclaimed photographic art gallery features the work of world-famous names like Anne Pigalle, Irving Penn and Hunter S. Thompson, and also nurtures new talent including Jeff Bark. The gallery's publishing division works with such luminaries as Terry Richardson.

Portobello Market

Portobello Road, W11. W: www.portobelloroad.co.uk Tube: Notting Hill Gate or Ladbroke Grove. Open: Sat approx 06:30-17:30

In addition to fashion and antiques, Portobello Market is also a good place to pick up works of art. Alongside stalls dealing in art and crafts, you'll find a cluster of fine art and sculpture galleries in the immediate area.

Riverside Studios

See the Riverside review featured above left.

WHITEWALL GALLERY

100 Westbourne Grove, W2 5RU. T: 020 7229 0952 W: www.whitewallgalleries.com Tube: Royal Oak Open: Tue-Thu 10:00-17:00, Fri-Sat 10:00-20:00 Sun 11:00-16:00

The Whitewall Gallery hit the headlines back in 2005 when Banksy famously released 200 live black rats into the space, for an exhibition he held here. Today, the contemporary art gallery features award-winning international artists, and occasionally hosts one-off exhibitions by external curators.

South London **review map**

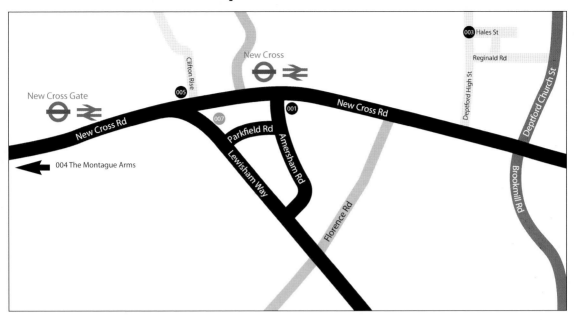

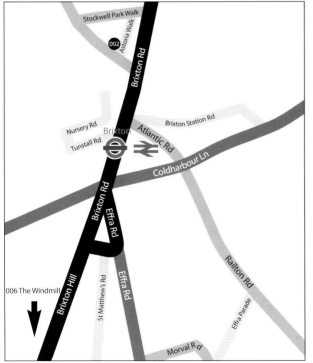

BARS & CLUBS

001 Amersham Arms: 388 New Cross Road. Page 128
002 Carling Academy Brixton: 211 Stockwell Road. Page 128
003 The Deptford Arms: 52 Deptford High Street. Page 128
004 The Montague Arms: 289 Queens Road. Page 129
005 New Cross Inn: 323 New Cross Road. Page 129
006 The Windmill: 22 Blenheim Gardens. Page 129

ART & CULTURE

007 New Cross Gallery: 3 Lewisham Way. Page 132

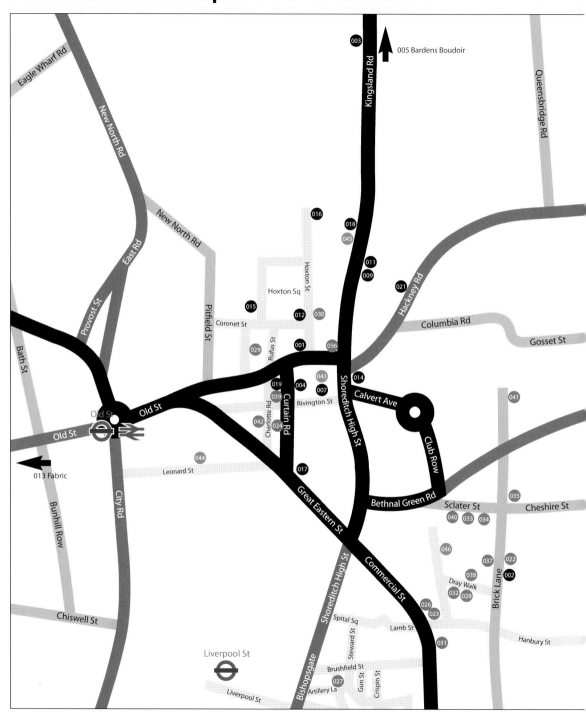

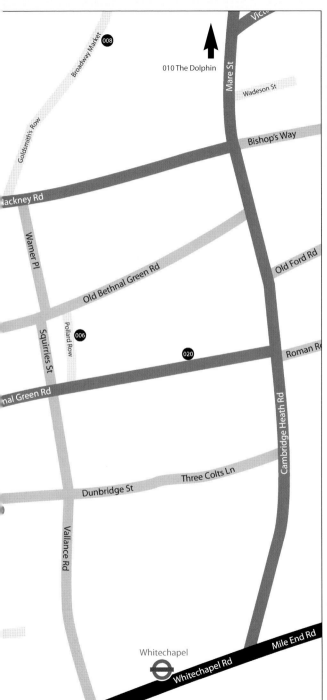

BARS & CLUBS

SHOPPING

ART & CULTURE

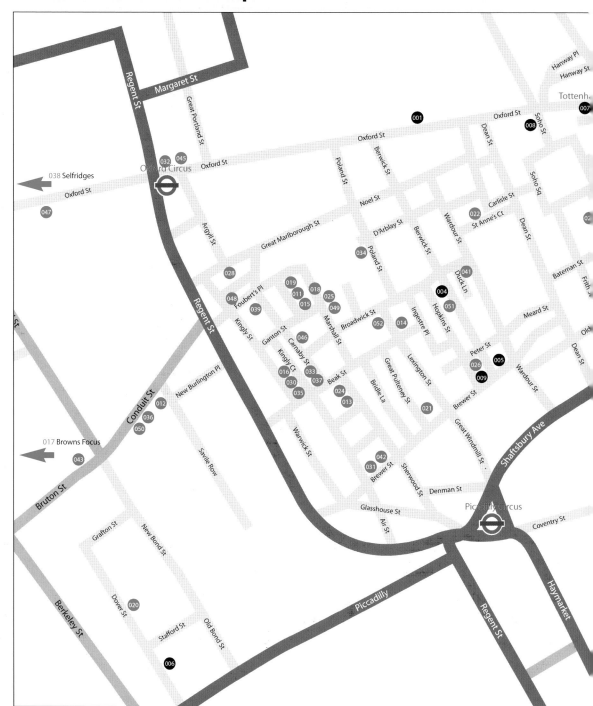

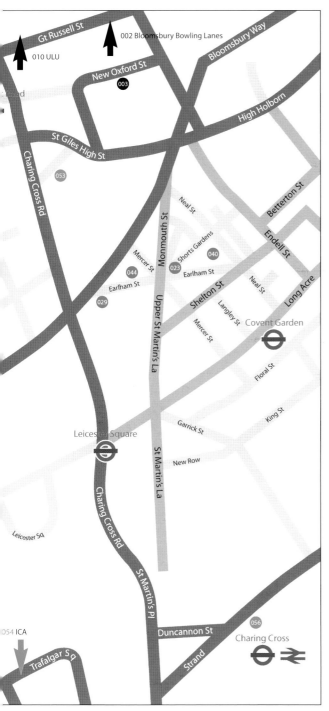

BARS & CLUBS

SHOPPING

ART & CULTURE

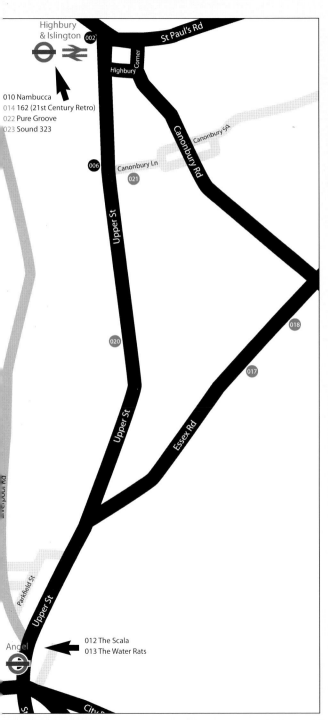

BARS & CLUBS

001   Barfly: 49 Chalk Farm Road. Page 111
002   The Buffalo Bar: 259 Upper Street. Page 111
003   The Dublin Castle: 94 Parkway. Page 111
004   The Enterprise: 2 Haverstock Hill. Page 112
005   The Good Mixer: 30 Inverness Street. Page 112
006   The Hope and Anchor: 207 Upper Street. Page 112
007   Koko: 1A Camden High Street. Page 114
008   The Lock Tavern: 35 Chalk Farm Road. Page 116
009   The Luminaire: 311 High Road. Page 116
010   Nambucca: 596 Holloway Road. Page 116
011   The Roundhouse: Chalk Farm Road. Page 116
012   The Scala: 275 Pentonville Road. Page 117
013   The Water Rats: 328 Grays Inn Road. Page 117

SHOPPING

014   162 (21st Century Retro): 162 Holloway Road. Page 122
015   Arckiv Eyewear: Stables Market, Chalk Farm Road. Page 122
016   Camden Stables Market: Chalk Farm Road. Page 122
017   Flashback: 50 Essex Road. Page 123
018   Haggle Vinyl: 114-116 Essex Road. Page 122
019   Know How Records: 3 Buck Street. Page 123
020   Labour of Love: 193 Upper Street. Page 123
021   Palette: 21 Canonbury Lane. Page 124
022   Pure Groove: 679 Holloway Road. Page 124
023   Sound 323: 323 Archway Road. Page 124

ART & CULTURE

024   atProud: Stables Market, Chalk Farm Road. Page 125

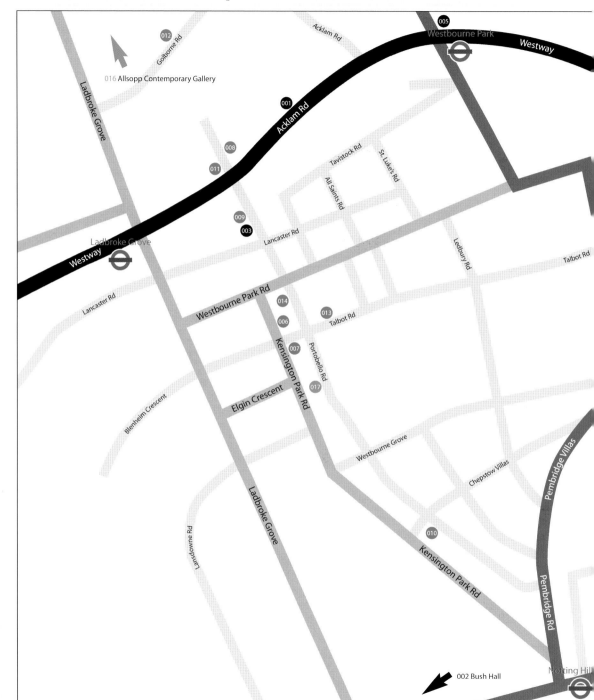

016 Allsopp Contemporary Gallery

002 Bush Hall

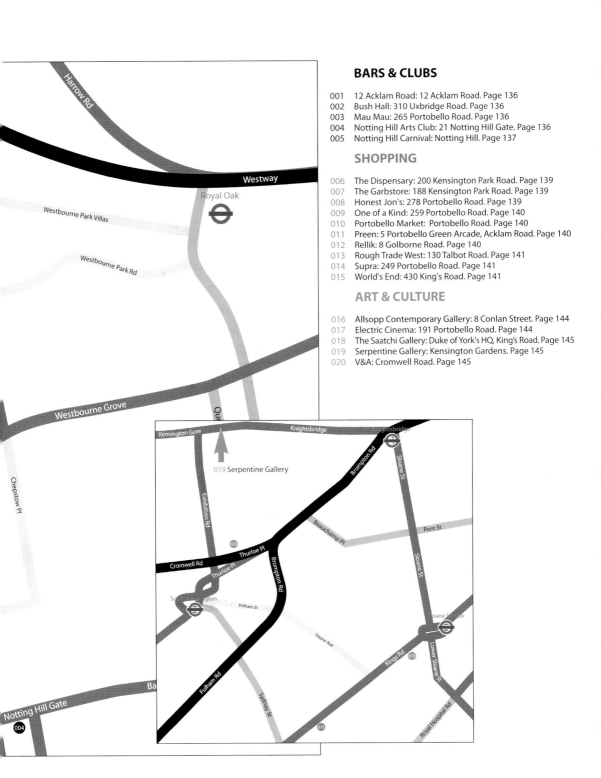

BARS & CLUBS

SHOPPING

ART & CULTURE

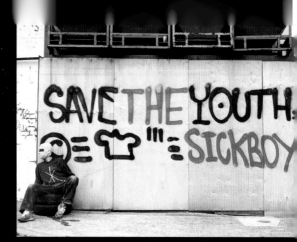